Spiritual Journey

Spiritual Journey

· ·

1,000 YOUNG ADULTS SHARE THE RECONCILING
EXPERIENCE OF TAIZÉ WITH THE
ARCHBISHOP OF CANTERBURY

George Carey

MOREHOUSE PUBLISHING

First published in Great Britain by Mowbray, a Cassell imprint, London

First U.S. edition published by
Morehouse Publishing
P.O. Box 1321
Harrisburg, PA 17105

First published 1994

Library of Congress Cataloging-in-Publication Data
Carey, George.
    A spiritual journey / George Carey.
      p. cm
    ISBN 0-8192-1595-3 (paper)
      1. Communauté de Taizé.   2. Christian pilgrims and pilgrimages—
France—Taizé.   3. Youth—Religious life.   4. Carey, George—
Journeys—France—Taizé.   5. Church of England—Bishops—Biography.
6. Anglican Communion—Bishops—Biography.   7. Taizé (France)—
Description and travel.   I. Title.
BV4408.C37 1994
271'.8—dc20   93-45516
                                                                      CIP

ISBN 0-8192-1595-3

Front cover: The Archbishop with one of the diocesan groups.
Back cover: The Archbishop with Brother Roger.
Both photographs © Ateliers et Presses de Taizé.

Typeset by Litho Link Ltd, Welshpool, Powys
Printed and bound in Great Britain by Mackays of Chatham PLC

Contents

Preface

....

Cardinal Suenens once remarked memorably 'It takes many to make one intelligent'. If that is so about a person's development, it is also true about the writing of a book. This book about Taizé has been shaped by a number of friends whose contributions have enriched my understanding of the spiritual life as well as helping to make it much better than it would otherwise have been.

I am grateful to Bishop Graham James, my former chaplain, for his considerable help with the text and to Bishop Peter Nott for liaising with the Taizé Community and adding anecdotal material which has strengthened the book. Canon Stephen Platten, Bishop Edward Holland and the Rev. Philip Dixon have also made most useful criticisms and suggestions which have improved my script. As always there are those without whom such books would never see the light of day and I have in mind the hard work of Canon Colin Fletcher, my present chaplain, and Mrs Ruth McCurry of Mowbray. In all this, my wife Eileen has been a constant encouragement and a useful sounding board.

But the two greatest influences on the book and the profound spiritual experience it expresses were the young people who came with me to Taizé and, of course, the Taizé Community itself. I can only thank God for the young whose openness to God remains an inspiration and challenge and for Brother Roger and the remarkable

Community to whom this book is dedicated. I hope the Community will feel that this book is an authentic expression of its life and in turn is a small 'thank you' for the ministry of love to all the Churches which like my tradition have been greatly blessed through its self-offering.

Introduction

....

Journey to Taizé

My journey to Taizé began in Canberra, Australia, some 9,000 miles away from the tiny village in central France where this book finds its inspiration. I was attending the seventh Assembly of the World Council of Churches in February 1991 as the Archbishop-designate of Canterbury. One evening I held a reception for other delegates. The guests provided a kaleidoscope of Christianity. My wife Eileen and I were fascinated to greet people from so many parts of the world. We were told stories of suffering in the Sudan, brave witness during the long years of Communism in Eastern Europe, renewal in Africa and Asia, and, at that time, worries about how Christians should respond to conflict in the Gulf. My mind and thoughts were darting from one concern to another when I found myself greeting a young man who introduced himself as Brother Emile from the Taizé Community.

'Oh', I exclaimed, 'I am so glad to meet you. Your community has had an amazing influence on all the churches in Britain. Thank you for all you are doing.' Emile smiled and said: 'I bring you greetings from Brother Roger and an invitation to you to visit the Community as soon as you can.' 'I will come', I said impulsively, 'on condition that I bring with me 1,000 young Anglicans!' Emile was not perturbed: 'We'd love that very much', he replied. So the idea was born. Like many good ideas it had to await its time.

I returned to England and was duly enthroned Archbishop of Canterbury on 19 April 1991. Although this was primarily an event in the life of the Church of England, once again I found myself amidst many friends from other churches and from the Anglican Communion around the world. It was a visual reminder of the immense opportunities as well as responsibilities of my new office. In my address I outlined my concern that our Church should be an open, accessible Church, sharing its faith with the world around. I expressed my dream of a Church 'renewed and invigorated, growing in faith and increasing in number; a Church united in its ambition to draw out a living faith in the young as well as in others and to involve lay people fully in its ministry and mission'.

Following my enthronement I continued to ponder about the Church's responsibility to reach young people. As I travelled around England I began to get a measure of the need and saw clear evidence of the Church's general failure to reach and nurture the young. I saw the large numbers of churches where no effective work among young people was going on. It seemed that only a minority of churches took Sunday schools seriously. Youth clubs were becoming an exception. And churches where there was a ministry for those under thirty were few indeed. With a sinking heart I heard evidence of an alarming gap between the young and the middle-aged in church life – a gap made palpably clear by youngsters who felt ignored by older Christians and who assumed that the Church of England was not for them. My concern focused on the questions: 'What can we do for young people? In what ways does the Church need to change in order to be the kind of community to which young people will want to belong?'

As I thought more about these questions I realized that a more personal question had to be faced: 'What can an Archbishop do?' I recognized that if I was not willing to take the initiative, I had little right to ask that others should do anything about it.

And so I remembered Brother Roger's invitation and my response in Canberra. What about a Youth Pilgrimage to Taizé? The idea returned full of new possibilities.

But why Taizé? What drew me to that place? The place is not special — but the people are. The Taizé Community was started some fifty years ago by a young Swiss. The Second World War led him to yearn for the reconciliation of the churches. In this reconciliation between Christians would be a sign of the reconciliation God willed for all his people. The young man with this vision was Roger Schutz-Marsauche. He had seen what war could do to human beings. It was not just the broken bodies which distressed him but the broken dreams of a new world order and the shattered hopes of peace that had been the pre-war dream. He had seen at first hand the terrors of Nazi-dominated Germany and he personally had helped many Jews to find eventual freedom by providing them with a hiding place. Brother Roger, as he became, still believes that true peace is only truly built on a genuinely spiritual life, in which God is honoured and prayer and worship are central.

So, having spent two years in Taizé on his own, Roger Schutz-Marsauche gathered around him a few like-minded friends who began to live as a community of prayer and worship. There was no 'rule' (the code by which a religious community orders its life) — that was to come later — but they lived in genuine co-operation and acceptance of one another. And they did not belong to one single Christian tradition, though in the early stages all came from churches of the Reformation. It was in the early 1960s that the first Anglicans joined the community. And then in 1969 came a new breakthrough: the first Roman Catholic joined the community. Since then many others have followed. Brother Roger's radically new approach to a religious community took time to build. He respected different Christian traditions but refused to see them as barriers. He wanted the genuine differences between Christians to be shared openly on the basis of a spiritual unity in God. There were, and this remains the case, no narrow loyalties at Taizé.

Perhaps this is the reason why the young have been drawn to Taizé in such numbers. Here Christian ideals, obscured in so many of our churches, are lived with conviction and joy. Brother Roger did not intend to create a community which would draw thousands of young people to join its life of prayer and worship. But he knew the future of Europe lay with the young. He wanted a better way than war. He wanted to show that life in the second half of the twentieth century could be lived with confidence in God. He wanted to demonstrate that Christianity was exciting, and that it held the key to a changed and transformed world.

But we still need to press the question: Why Taizé for my pilgrimage? I must answer that personally. I had never been to Taizé, yet it held a fascination for me ever since a young lady from St Nicholas Church in Durham (where I was vicar in the 1970s) came back transformed by the experience. Her prayer life was quite wonderfully changed and deepened. When she was asked by some of her friends the reason, she would brush her hair from her eyes and exclaim: 'Taizé is so difficult to *explain*; you must go and *experience!*'

An even deeper motivation was my strong feeling that Christian work among young people must be rooted in the spiritual life. To be candid, my deepest worry about the 'Decade of Evangelism' was, and remains, the danger of it becoming superficial and ending up as a process designed merely to recruit membership for the Church. For me evangelism is about people meeting, finding and growing in God. There were many who had met and found God at Taizé. There was no need to create something new, and I had no wish to re-invent the wheel. Meeting, finding and growing in God is an act of pilgrimage, and since Taizé was not identified with any particular church or tradition, it had widespread appeal. The Evangelical as well as the Catholic feels at home there. It is not associated with any of the controversies of the past. So Taizé became my choice for this pilgrimage with the young. And how right it turned out to be.

But first I had to interest my brother bishops in the idea. Despite what many believe, the Archbishop of Canterbury cannot tell the bishops what to do. There is great freedom in the Church of England — one of its most creative features, even if it makes the Church sometimes slow to move. I wrote to all the diocesan bishops in August 1991 telling them that I planned to visit Taizé the following August and that it was my wish to take a thousand young Anglicans with me. I decided to target the 17–25 age group, since young adults are those most absent from our congregations. I asked the bishops to send twenty young people from each of their dioceses and to appoint a diocesan co-ordinator to be a link with Lambeth. I wanted to lead a pilgrimage truly representative of the whole of the Church of England.

Every bishop responded positively. That was a sign of blessing (I dare not say miracle!) in itself. We held a meeting for all the co-ordinators at Lambeth Palace. Some bishops had appointed their diocesan youth officers as co-ordinators; others had not. But it was the youth officers who had most to say at the meeting. It was clear that some had misgivings about this pilgrimage, not least because I had gone ahead in planning without consulting them in advance. But I had wanted to get the bishops to back this pilgrimage and so I had gone directly to them. I had also wanted to make it clear that an Archbishop ought to be in direct contact with young people in the Church, and that this pilgrimage would, as far as possible, be a chance for personal encounter. I did not want simply to be a figure-head.

But if I was surprised by this reaction, I was in for a shock as well. My family had made our holiday plans to be near Taizé so we would be on hand to welcome the young pilgrims during the last week in August. But the co-ordinators believed that the pilgrimage should start with everyone meeting at Canterbury Cathedral for a service before we made our way to Taizé! This turned out to be an excellent idea even though it meant that my wife and I had to drive some 450 miles from Burgundy the day before to get to Canterbury before returning to the same area of France. I was glad to do it, though, because it did emphasize further the theme of pilgrimage. At our meeting at Lambeth I described to the co-ordinators my vision of this pilgrimage.

Pilgrimage appeals to me because it is centred on movement. Everyone will come from a different part of the country, and though we may travel in our separate coaches, and cross the Channel on different ferries, we will be travelling in the same direction. That is a parable of the Christian life. We come from different backgrounds, have different experiences, and each begin our Christian journey at different points and in different places, but our goal is the same — unity in Christ with one another, life in the kingdom of God.

I went on to describe my own personal aim in this pilgrimage. As I look at these words, I marvel at how wonderfully they were fulfilled in the event:

I want to stress that I am going to Taizé as a *fellow pilgrim alongside young people*, to learn something about what others have found there and simply to wait on God with them. The ministry I want to exercise at Taizé is less a ministry *to* the young than a ministry *with* the young. And so my days at Taizé will be very much like theirs. We shall have a time each day when our groups will gather together, and sometimes I shall speak to everyone, seeking to explore the nature of the Christian faith. But I shall also want simply to be with the young people as they pray and learn. I will be a fellow pilgrim with them.

The months went by. Some dioceses took longer than others to produce their young people. The logistical planning took up many hours of staff time at Lambeth and in the offices of Nuneaton Coaches, who organized the transport. Eventually on a sunny late August Saturday we found ourselves in Canterbury Cathedral for the service to begin our pilgrimage. Young people had themselves devised the worship which was prayerful, inspiring, encouraging, thoughtful and fun. From the beginning it was clear that these young people had come determined to have a good time. What cheered me was to see the great range of people in the cathedral. I had insisted on the widest range of participation. I wanted people from the inner cities, from rural areas, from different ethnic communities; employed and unemployed, students and young marrieds; the disabled too. In my short address to them I told them what I hoped we would discover on our pilgrimage together.

I have never been to Taizé. Nor, I believe, have most of you. So we shall be on a pilgrimage of discovery together. I want to go to Taizé because I know it is a place which has changed and transformed the Christian lives of countless people, especially the young. I hope I am not too old to catch its spirit! Archbishops are often expected to know all the answers to questions of faith. But Taizé is a place for the seeker after truth, the searcher after God and in this life our Christian pilgrimage is never complete. An Archbishop must never forget that he is a seeker and a searcher after truth. And I want to do that searching at Taizé alongside those of you in the first years of your adult Christian lives.

I hoped that reassured them that as Archbishop I was not going with presuppositions that might restrict their growth; I wished to learn from them too. I went on to say that in sharing the journey with them it was my intention to meet them in their diocesan groups each day and to share our experiences as we went along.

And so eighteen coaches rolled out of Canterbury late that evening full of excited and expectant young men and women who were determined to enjoy their Christian faith and to set out on an adventure of learning more about their Lord and their faith. Six other coaches were on their way directly to Taizé. The pilgrimage had begun.

As I made my own way to Taizé I started to reflect about the place of young people in the Church. Already I had caught the spirit of those young people and felt the energy and vitality of their faith and hope. Why is it that we have so often failed to channel their enthusiasm in the life of the churches? I recalled meeting a young man years ago who was handing out Communist literature in London. I knew he had grown up in a believing Christian home. 'Why have you ceased to call yourself a Christian?' I asked. His reply was definite: 'I wanted something to believe in that would grasp me intellectually and emotionally and something that would demand everything from me. I did not find that in Christianity.' I still recall the shock and disappointment of that reply and my mind flashed to the commanding words of Jesus to his disciples: 'Take up your cross and follow me.' I wondered then and wonder now how the excitement of the world- and Christ-affirming message of Christianity has been emasculated by so many of us and become a tired and dispirited travesty of a world-transforming faith. 'How may these dry bones live?' is perhaps the most urgent question facing all the churches today. It is a question which goes well beyond the cry to be relevant. There is no evidence that faith stripped of the miraculous is what people want or need. If we have learned anything over the last fifty years it is surely that a gospel which fails to proclaim the wonder, majesty and glory of God has no power to lead people to him. But this is no cry for fundamentalism. If people reject a slimmed-down faith made acceptable, they equally despise a naïve and intolerant faith which fails to take their questions seriously.

As we made the journey from Canterbury to Taizé I thought of the two different places they represented. I was going from one place of pilgrimage to another. Canterbury — a place which still pulsates with the enduring memory of the mission of St Augustine to the Anglo-Saxons, a mission rooted in the monastic tradition of contemplation and prayer. That mission was founded in the simple obedience of monks who were compelled by their faith to share it with others. But Canterbury is also dominated by another memory. In 1170 Thomas Becket, Archbishop of Canterbury, was brutally murdered by four knights who believed they were doing the will of Henry II: a vivid reminder that following Christ takes the Church into conflict with earthly powers. As a result of that martyrdom Canterbury became the most important pilgrimage centre of the mediaeval world; a story immortalized in Chaucer's great *Canterbury Tales*. Even today modern pilgrims come, drawn by the power of faith so evident in the story of the building itself.

The story of Taizé is also a tale of faith, sacrifice and love. As a young man in the war Roger Schutz-Marsauche felt a strong compulsion to found a Christian community and as an act of faith was led to buy a run-down house in the poor village of Taizé, in Burgundy. In the autumn of 1944 Roger and his three prospective brothers moved to the house and their work of reconciliation began. 'Reconciliation', Brother Roger was to say to me, 'was there from the start. The key verse was John 17.21, "that they all may be one: as thou, Father, art in me, and I in thee". Reconciliation between Christians, between all people . . .' That still remains the goal of Taizé and from those tiny precarious beginnings the community has grown from four brothers to a hundred men who have devoted their lives to Christ's task of bringing peace and reconciliation to others.

To this other place of pilgrimage, then, almost a

thousand English pilgrims were wending their way, many of them young idealists looking for new directions and seeking to find the living God and his will for their lives. What would they discover and what would prayer and quietness mean for them? In what ways would they be challenged by the life of the community and be changed by the pilgrimage?

In the chapters that follow we trace the journey that many of them took. My reflections have been very profoundly influenced by the many conversations that arose from encounters with these young people each day. This book is as much their book as it is mine. We grew together in our knowledge and love of God.

One

....

Journey into prayer

The English pilgrims arrived at Taizé from Sunday lunchtime onwards. My wife Eileen and I arrived just after noon, accompanied by the Bishop of Norwich, the Rt Rev. Peter Nott (who had been greatly influenced by Taizé when a young man, and who was still closely associated with the Community) and the Rt Rev. Edward Holland, the suffragan Bishop in Europe. The diocese of Gibraltar-in-Europe is part of the Church of England and covers a vast area. Once made up simply of chaplaincies to English people living abroad, it has now developed a life and ethos of its own. It too had sent young people to Taizé but they had not joined us at Canterbury, coming as they did in ones and twos from places as far apart as Madrid, Oslo and Athens. Also with my party were two close colleagues — my chaplain, Graham James, and my secretary for ecumenical affairs, Stephen Platten.

To my great astonishment Brother Roger and the whole Taizé Community were waiting on the road to receive me. I had expected no formal greeting and didn't want any great fuss. I soon discovered that this was simply to be the last short step of my pilgrimage to Taizé and the first step of a journey into 'the prayer' which lies at the heart of Taizé. I noticed that the brothers often referred to the round of daily worship as 'the Prayer'.

Brother Roger is a man of medium height, slim, and generally clad in a simple white robe. He greeted me with a shy smile. From the gate of the community house the brothers led us up to the church singing the well-known Taizé song 'Laudate Dominum' ('Praise the Lord') as they went. There we were greeted by many hundreds of other worshippers. In the quietness of the huge Church of Reconciliation we knelt to ask God's blessing on this pilgrimage of young Anglicans to Taizé.

At lunch Brother Roger apologized for his poor English and I was able to reciprocate for my poor French! But language is never a problem for long for fellow Christians. We began to converse with each other helped by a young brother, Matthew, who spoke with a Yorkshire accent. I discovered that Matthew came from Pudsey. He was an Anglican. So too were seven or eight other brothers. I was glad to discover this, yet as time went on, it became less and less important. These men were simply Taizé brothers, united in common worship, prayer and service. Roger explained that though there had been other Christian leaders, including two previous Archbishops of Canterbury, who had been to Taizé, no other leader had led such a large group for such a length of time. He believed that this was significant for the Church.

Roger viewed the task of the Church from the vantage point of Taizé which had its own network of communication on every continent; he was both heartened and concerned for the body of Christ throughout the world — concerned for 'the continuity of Christ in the human family', as he often puts it. He could see the challenge of a secularized Europe.

He spoke of the many villages around Taizé where churches are no longer in use. When he arrived here over fifty years ago, the village church of Taizé had been disused since the French Revolution at the end of the eighteenth century. There had been a 'winter of the Church'. But Brother Roger could also see great changes within the space of a single generation. In the surrounding region, the anti-clericalism of former times had greatly diminished. In addition, he underlined how the Catholic Church in France had very fine bishops with great pastoral understanding. Although the priests in the region are not numerous, they are excellent. And there are very committed lay people. In the surrounding villages, it is often lay people who preside at burials.

'Where is the hope?' I asked. He gesticulated in the direction of the young brothers standing nearby and towards a band of young pilgrims, laughing in the distance. 'That is the hope of the Church', he said, 'the young. They have the capacity to see Christ and follow him. When they find the meaning of their lives in the risen Christ, they have the capacity to change the world. Yet let us not forget either that there are older people too, sometimes well on in years, who know how to communicate around themselves an immense hope for the future.'

Our conversation was interrupted by the arrival of the first of the twenty-four English coaches which roared up the narrow lane through the tiny village of Taizé and parked in the arrival area. Out poured the tired but excited young people who after some fourteen hours in coaches were glad to arrive at their destination. They were directed to their quarters. Some slept in their own tents. Others were in dormitories or were given tents. It seemed chaotic, yet a sense of calm purpose prevailed. Our pilgrims were delighted to be here at last. Our pilgrimage had begun.

Strictly speaking a pilgrimage is a journey to a place sanctified by a saint or a holy martyr. Canterbury from which we had come was such a place. T.S. Eliot in *Murder in the Cathedral* puts it powerfully: 'Wherever a saint has dwelt, wherever a martyr has given his blood for the blood of Christ, there is holy ground and the sanctity shall not depart from it.' Taizé, of course, does not fall into that category, even though its roots were planted firmly in the blood, tears and suffering of the Second World War. Instead it has become a place of pilgrimage through the presence of the community and their living witness to a reconciled Church. It has become a place 'where prayer has been valid'. Although it had no long history of pilgrimage and no blood of martyrs, it has acquired a deep sanctity through an impressive devotion to Christ. It particularly appeals to young people.

For thousands of people who have undertaken this journey to Taizé what has most transformed them there has been prayer. Taizé is *prayer*. What did I and others learn about prayer through this visit to Taizé?

The first thing most of us encounter when we spend any length of time trying to pray is the problem of bringing our lives under a new discipline. Modern people rush to get anywhere. If 'nature abhors a vacuum', it is certainly true that for most of us there is no space in our lives. Our day starts in a rush and usually ends in one. Even people who pray daily tend to squeeze prayer into slots of time. It is as if we say to God: 'Sorry, that is all I can spare — ten minutes at 7.50 a.m. — and then I'm off.' I thought I could pride myself on being very disciplined and that I spent more time than the average person — even the average priest — in prayer. After all, did I not have a regular discipline of Bible study followed by the daily office in Lambeth Palace Chapel? Yes, I did, but I found that I had much to learn about prayer because I too, like a commando, 'hit the ground running'. I too squeezed prayer into slots in an over-busy diary.

'The Prayer' at Taizé is marked by simplicity. There are three services in church each day; at 8.00 in the morning, at noon and in the evening. Each follows much the same pattern. The structure of the liturgy is reassuringly simple. Short passages of Scripture and brief prayers based on common themes are interwoven with the refrain of Taizé songs. Every service has a ten-minute period of silence, which seemed long at the beginning of the week and not long enough by the end.

What did we English pilgrims learn about prayer?

Each day I met up with our young people, in groups of about forty or fifty. It was a time for open exchange. The informality of Taizé and the directness of young people broke through any artificial barriers between us. It seemed the most natural thing in the world to talk about God in the warm air of the Burgundian countryside. Early in the week we talked about *distractions*. 'At first I found it so difficult to pray because of so many distractions. I don't mean from outside but from within', said one girl. 'I found myself thinking about my boyfriend and what he might be doing now.' And others chimed in: 'I found myself day-dreaming.' 'It was boring.' 'I was thinking of my summer holidays.' 'I found it difficult to hold one thought in my head.'

Their thoughts reflected my own. Like Martha in the gospel I was occupied with much that had very little to do with the Lord. I was thinking about my future programme when I returned from Taizé — particularly the coming debate on the ordination of women! But there were also the distractions of my fellow worshippers in the huge church. At any service there might be 4,000 people. Their coughs and splutters, their shuffling into place caught my ears and eyes. But the distractions include bodily discomfort. I used a prayer stool during my time at Taizé and sometimes my back would ache or a leg would go to sleep. 'How, Lord' I wondered, 'can you expect us to pray when our bodies are so uncomfortable?' I began to see that the worst distraction in prayer was myself!

How should we deal with distractions? At Taizé gradually I found my own method of handling them. I would spend the first few minutes of my prayer time allowing any thoughts at all to enter my mind. I would invite distractions as the first stage of my praying. Instead of being 'distractions', therefore, I was treating them as part of the person I am. A few actual examples may assist. On the second morning at Taizé into my mind came four independent and rather irritating problems. One was a family matter concerning one of our children; then there was a staff problem at Lambeth; there was the prospect of a visit to the Ecumenical Patriarch in Istanbul; finally there was a general worry about the pressure of work. My attention was drawn to the many candles flickering in the semi-darkness at the front of the church. I decided to make those candles my focus for handling the distractions. I began half reflecting and half praying. Words formed in my mind: 'Lord, lights gather extra brilliance and strength from proximity with one another. As I am here in this place with so many Christians around me, give me light as I bring to you these difficulties.' And one by one, I examined briefly the different problems before God and weighed up the different options open to me. After a short while I was able to move outwards from my immediate concerns to wider issues in prayer. The essential feature of this way of dealing with wandering thoughts is that they are treated not as alien to us but as part of the people we are and thus integral to our praying. Thus included, the rest of our prayers can be ordered.

The things that distract us are usually the things most on our minds. If we attempt to suppress what troubles us most when we come before God, we will never enter into a honest relationship with him. He is not fooled, of course, but we are fooling ourselves if we present to him only what is good and ordered and whole in our lives. The closest relationships are established by trust and honesty. The same is true in our relationship with God in prayer. I may not have received clear answers to the problems and worries I brought before God at Taizé, but their burden was lightened. He had taken part of that load, as he always does through the welcoming arms of his Son, held open for us on the cross.

As I prayed at Taizé I noticed that a number of young brothers in the community lay prostrate during the time of silence, their heads touching the ground. What can they be praying?, I found myself wondering. They seemed to have a communion with God that dwarfed my present experience. I was intrigued and impressed by their capacity to go beyond the self-consciousness that often inhibits true prayer. Here, I reminded myself, is another type of distraction: comparing myself with others. It is not for us to wonder about the prayer lives of fellow Christians. Our task is to seek the living God with all our hearts.

My time at Taizé gave me space to re-learn five valuable things about prayer.

First, prayer is *waiting*. Don't be in too much of a hurry when you pray. Be still and enter his presence as you would if you were going to the home of a dear and honoured friend. You may have business to transact but such is the friendship that there is no rush to get around to it. Friendship is too precious to be rushed; it is to be enjoyed. Prayer is like that. We should learn the art of prayer-friendship. In this time we may want to express to God how much we love him; how unworthy we are to be counted as his friends; how grateful we are for his many blessings in this life; for the love of others and for the graces of life we so often take for granted. Sometimes what I do is to mention the many graces I had received that very day: 'For the gift of life, for the love and support of a dear wife, for the life and vigour of this community and especially for Brother Roger on my right as he prays . . .'

Many of the songs and chants at Taizé explore this theme of 'waiting'. 'Wait for the Lord . . .' was frequently sung during our week there. This haunting melody still echoes in my mind. I know some Christians who find this dimension of Taizé disturbing. What are we waiting for? Christ has come. He has died. He is risen. He is alive today. Why then do we have to wait?

What we are waiting for is the coming of his kingdom. The Church has always been caught in the 'between-time', between Christ's first coming and the completion of his work when his will is done 'on earth as in heaven'. All our prayers are uttered in this 'between-time', because we live in it. The whole Christian life is characterized by waiting. Indeed, one of the most impressive Anglican thinkers of our day, W.H. Vanstone, has explored this theme in his book *The Stature of Waiting*. Vanstone shows how much the theme of 'waiting' features in the New Testament and how central it was to the life and ministry of Jesus himself. So prayer that never gets beyond the stage of waiting is still valid prayer, perhaps the style of prayer most like that of Jesus himself, who waited in Gethsemane and invites us, his disciples, to 'watch and pray' with him.

For one of our young pilgrims, Carolyn from the west of England, waiting is a reality which has made her more aware of the mystery of suffering. Just nineteen years of age, she suffers from multiple sclerosis and came to Taizé in a wheelchair. She asked us to pray for her in the lovely Orthodox chapel adjacent to the main church building. She poured out her agony and longing for wholeness; she confessed her fears and worries. Together we talked and prayed and kept silent. For Carolyn waiting meant acceptance that she probably would not get better and most possibly would get worse. Her journey is one that very few of us could cope with, but Carolyn's willingness to say 'Not my will but thine be done' was a wonderful example of a young person's mature faith.

It is clear from Carolyn's experience that prayer is a *relationship*. Prayer never exists in isolation. It flows from a relationship with God. That wonderful but much misunderstood word 'fellowship' sums it up. I know that many people pray who have no connection with the Church; I'm sure there are others who pray who have very little knowledge of God. Such prayer, honourable and good though it is, falls short of Christian prayer. Christian prayer finds its origin in God's love for us expressed in Jesus Christ. It flows from our relationship with him. Because we are his children we can enter his presence crying: 'Abba! Father!' (Gal 4.6).

All relationships have to be worked at in order to survive.

The reason why many marriages collapse is because that this obvious truth is ignored. Physical beauty and sexual attraction are insecure foundations for lifelong relationships. What will hold people together is a love built on friendship and cemented by daily contact, frank and fresh talking, and the constant holding of hands and touching of lives. These are elements of 'prayer'. Our friendship with Almighty God depends on us maintaining communion with him, allowing our lives to touch his. This God, who has revealed himself to us in Jesus his Son, longs for us to spend time with him. We need to spend time daily in his company.

If we remember that prayer presupposes a deep and trusting relationship we already have with God through Jesus our Lord, it will help us through the tough times when prayer may seem like running through sand.

Bishop Peter Nott told us all a delightful story of an encounter with a young American during our week at Taizé. The young man, Michael, asked Peter if he could spare time for a talk. He said that he had heard so much about the community and what it meant for so many young people, he had saved up and made the trip. He expected it all to be marvellous and uplifting and a great spiritual experience. He tried to pray during the services and it just didn't work for him: 'It's no good. I can't pray.'

'How long have you been here?' asked Bishop Peter. 'It's my first day', he said. Peter then related to him his own experience a year before when he had returned to Taizé after a gap of about twenty years. He was excited about coming back to a place which had been such a blessing when he had been a young priest. But to his dismay he found that he couldn't pray. Like the young man, he tried hard but it was no good. So he stopped trying and made no attempt to form words in his mind. He said: 'I just rested and did nothing.' Then, said Peter to the American, after a while a sense of the presence of God began to creep in and little by little, Peter was caught up in the worship — almost as if he was being carried by others. And then he found he could pray — but the prayer was more peaceful, more restful and more trustful.

'So you are not alone', said the bishop to the young man: 'Do nothing. Just rest and stop making efforts. Stop *trying* to pray and you will find that God will come to you because that is what this place is all about — receiving the gift of God.'

Bishop Peter said to me later: 'As you know, there were about 5,000 people in Taizé during our week and finding individual people was like finding a needle in a haystack. But through one of the little miracles that seems to happen there, two evenings later I bumped into Michael. He was walking with two friends laughing and chatting happily. "How's life, Michael?" I asked. He beamed: "Great!" he replied. "You were right — I just rested and it all came good."'

And the space that Taizé provided gave us all time to be with God. Not only in the church during our times of common prayer but when we walked from place to place.

Third, prayer is *dialogue*. 'How does God speak to us?' one of our pilgrims asked me. I could only answer him out of my own experience. I have already mentioned that Bible study is part of my discipline. That is for me a rich reservoir of ideas and thoughts. As it happened I was able to give him a specific reply. Only that morning I had been reading Exodus 23 and I had been struck by verse 30: 'Little by little I will drive them out from before you until you are increased and possess the land'. The writer was talking about the tribes of Israel entering the Promised Land. God was promising to drive out the Canaanites and other dwellers of the land but he was not going to do it at once; it would be 'little by little'. Every part of Scripture has a primary readership. In this case it was written for the Israelites. Yet we can see a word from the Lord for our own time and situation. I remarked to the young pilgrim that the passage spoke to the impulsive and impatient side of me. God's way is often to do things gradually. He moves at the pace that matches our ability to deal with the situation. So here was a promise which he and I could claim. 'Little by little.' It is as if God is saying to us: 'Don't despair; work patiently, purposefully and you will inherit the land.'

But God may speak to us through familiar words in the liturgy or even through words of hymns or songs. One of our young pilgrims remarked that for her the simple chants sung by the Community were fitting to be used in conversation with God. Although we shall look at Taizé music later, I found some of her examples helpful. She mentioned two of her favourite songs: 'Laudate omnes gentes' — 'Sing praises all you peoples, sing praises to the Lord'. 'As I sing it', she said, 'I am inviting God to hear my praise for him. I sing it with joy.' Her other favourite was 'Stay with us Lord'. The words are: 'Stay with us, O Lord Jesus Christ, night will soon fall. Then stay with us, O Lord Jesus Christ, light in our darkness.' She explained that her own prayers could form around such songs as these. She took comfort that the light of Christ overcomes all the darkness around her and within.

I know that many people find the idea of prayer *as dialogue* difficult because, they say, 'I talk to God but he never speaks back'. This, though, ignores the rich reservoir of Scripture, tradition and the record of people's experience

Leaving Canterbury (© Jim Rosenthal)

The English group arrives (© William Clemmey)

A meal is served (© Ateliers et Presses de Taizé)

At supper with the Taizé brothers (© Ateliers et Presses de Taizé)

of God which other Christians have written for our benefit. He is in constant dialogue with the world. But we have to *listen* to him.

This leads into another feature of prayer — one that is much neglected — that of prayer as *listening*. Too often we approach prayer as if we must be the active partners and that God is passive. That's not true. In the Gospels Jesus often goes off 'to a lonely place to pray'. He goes to be in communion with God. He too needs to listen to his Father.

Listening is an art. It demands attention. I like to call it 'the art of loving attention'. When you visit someone in hospital you might sit by the bedside and, after a few words, you realize that there is little of importance to be said. The patient may be too ill to speak to you. But you remain, listening, full of loving attention to that person.

Our loving attention to God is part of the quality of listening in prayer. A renewed awareness of the beauty of creation can come with loving attention at sunrise. A changed understanding of God's mysterious presence in suffering can come with the loving attention to the sick. A different perspective on God's care for children can come with loving attention to their questions and observations about his world. 'Does God grow?' asked a child one day, taking me into realms of thought I had hitherto only explored academically in what is called 'process theology'. It was that child's concept of God growing to embrace all the suffering and joys of the world that spoke to me, leading me to contemplate that, yes, the nature of love and especially his love on the cross must mean that God must be changed through encounter with his creation.

Meditation is often confused with prayer or understood as if it is the whole of prayer. But prayer as *meditation* came alive for me at Taizé. Meditation is often a difficult thing for modern people in a hurry. I asked Brother Roger what meditation meant for him. He thought for a minute and then said that meditation for him has to be centred on Christ. Although techniques of prayer undoubtedly help people, it is not *what* you *do* that matters but *who* is the centre of devotion.

Central to Taizé's spirituality is devotion to Christ. Taizé is a place of prayer for so many traditions that the nature of the Church is not a topic of debate or major enquiry. Both the Evangelical and Catholic dimensions find their focus in the Lordship of Christ. It was natural therefore for Roger to make Christ the centre of meditation. The ministry of Christ is an excellent place to begin to learn the art of meditation.

We might begin by considering the life of Jesus Christ and meditating on his sufferings as a human being. That he knew temptation as we do; that he knew what it was to go hungry, to be discouraged, to be maligned and treated badly, to be lonely and forgotten. Often a crucifix or a cross in a church building or in our room will be a focus of meditation as we dwell on the incredible sufferings of Christ for us.

I often find myself going back to some of the sayings of Christ in the gospels. Here are a few that have nourished me. The '*I am*' sayings — '*I am* the bread of life', '*I am* the way, the truth and the life', '*I am* the door of the sheepfold'. This is a rich vein for reflection. Take the first one. In what way is Jesus still the bread of life for me today? How do I feed on him and how am I nourished by him? And this may lead on to some simple prayers which may take a form like this: 'Lord, I want to thank you that you are still the living Bread from heaven. Feed me today and evermore. Lord, I adore you that your gospel still reaches hungry people. Be with me in my ministry today that I may feed those who come to me in your name . . .'

Christian meditation is an entering into the mind and will of Christ. When he meditated, he meditated upon the will of his heavenly Father. So may we when we enter into his prayer. That's why so often at Taizé it is the direct yet simple sayings of our Lord in John's Gospel that are repeated, almost epigrammatically.

Waiting, relationship, dialogue, listening and meditation: these are the words and themes that Taizé left with me. It was a surprise since I expected to learn more about technique in prayer. What I discovered instead was about the depth and range of prayer itself.

Not that technique is despised at Taizé. It is not. I mentioned earlier that as I was praying in the Church of Reconciliation I could see that some of the young brothers were prostrate, their heads touching the ground. This reminds us that posture can aid prayer greatly. Kneeling or lying prostrate is for many of us a fitting position for penitence as we say 'Sorry', asking for forgiveness. Standing with hands raised high will be for some an evocative position for prayer, favoured it seems by the Psalmist. At Taizé I was presented with a prayer stool and I find it a most helpful way of praying, as long as you get one that does not cut into the back of your legs!

But you don't have to go to church to pray. Walking too can be used greatly for prayer. As you walk to work you can use the regularity of your pace to say, for example, the Jesus Prayer: 'Lord, have mercy on me a sinner' —

repeating a phrase, or just the name of Jesus, until you start to live and breathe it. Or if you have a good memory the rhythm of walking may be conducive for singing under your breath a familiar hymn or modern song. Instead of daydreaming and fantasizing, which most people do when they are walking, use it to the glory of God and to intercede for God's Church.

But a focus can help in prayer as well. At Taizé I found the lights helped me to focus on Jesus as the Light of the world. For some it might also be a cross or a picture or an 'icon'. In my chapel at Lambeth over the altar there is a fine picture of the 'face' of Christ. I often use it as a focus of meditation. I might say something like this as I meditate upon the eyes, mouth and ears of our Lord: 'Help me, O Lord, to look with your gaze at the people I shall meet today. Help me to consider them as people greatly loved by you and therefore by me.' 'In the days of your flesh you spoke with power and grace to all who heard you. May I speak with your authority this day.' 'Lord, you listened with great care and sympathy to the cries of the poor and helpless. You were aware of the touch of the needy and the pleading glances of the distressed. Open my ears today to listen with great care to the agonies of your world.'

There are aids to prayer all around us. That's because we live in God's world. And when we live with him and for him, it shines with a new light. For praying is living with God just as he lives with us.

Two

....

Journey into the unexpected

The first strange thing you encounter at Taizé is the makeshift character of the place. The Community has now existed for fifty years, and people have been coming in their thousands for decades. Yet everything seems strangely impermanent, curiously insubstantial. The instinct of the Christian Church to build grand cathedrals or impressive monasteries as a mark of success has been avoided. At Taizé pilgrims are reminded that the whole Christian life is a pilgrimage. 'Here we have no continuing city, but we seek the one to come.'

The next strange thing to strike newcomers is that they will have to share their life at Taizé with strangers. Our young people did not remain together as a single group. They were distributed to different tents and dormitories, and had to face immediately the task of getting on with others of different nationality, ethnic background and language. The strangeness contained in the diversity of the human family quickly becomes apparent at Taizé. But under the warm Burgundy sun there is a daily discovery of a strange yet deep unity in Christ.

The accommodation at Taizé shares the same quality of impermanence. It is basic and simple; no attempt is made to bring accommodation up to the standards that one might look for on the kind of holidays that Britons usually expect and demand. Everything is clean and wholesome but the unspoken message is 'You are not on holiday; you are on a pilgrimage to meet God. Don't worry about things; relax and trust in the Lord.' The brothers themselves live in a group of houses in the village about 200 metres away from the Church of Reconciliation. Their accommodation is correspondingly simple. Brother Roger wanted me and my immediate party to live with them, so we occupied a house in which a group of brothers usually lived. This was partly to give me the chance to get to know Roger and the community and for them to have access to me each day. As well as his devotion to silence, I soon discovered that Roger was keen to talk at length about world-wide Christianity. And he was a generous host. Daily we had lunch and dinner with the community in the open air under the trees. The meals were always very basic but nourishing. Looking around at the laughing brothers of all ages as they relaxed over their meal I could not but be struck by their obvious contentment in their calling and their joy in serving the Lord.

But I was also struck by the great variety of the brothers. They represented many different ethnic groups and traditions. In themselves they were a rich cross-section of the Christian Church: Catholic, Anglican, Lutheran and Reformed. The diversity and range of professional gifts was very noticeable and impressive — accountants, teachers, printers, professors, computer programmers, medical students through to theologians, they testified to the way God was able to call everyone to himself.

I asked Roger how the community was able to hold diversity and unity together. 'What lessons are here', I asked, 'for the wider Church? We desperately need to find ways of offering our richness in diversity to each other and to discover our unity within it.'

Roger took me back into the history of the Community he had started here in 1940. In 1944, he and the first three brothers who had joined him in Geneva, Max Thurian, Pierre Souverain and Daniel de Montmollin, moved back to the house in Taizé. Their commitment was to a common life of prayer and work which would be anchored in celibacy and the sharing of material possessions. Roger explained that no carefully worked-out Rule had then been devised. They simply felt that a small number of Christians ready to commit their lives to reconciliation could move mountains of indifference, but how that would happen they were not sure.

They began by caring for those who were destitute. Initially during the war, while Brother Roger was still alone, he had sheltered political refugees fleeing from Nazism, especially Jews. This caused many difficulties for him and he was denounced to the police. In the summer of 1942, he was advised to leave Taizé because his life was in danger. He had no wish to leave but he had to stop welcoming people to his home so as not to place them in danger. In November 1942, just as the whole of France was occupied, the Gestapo, the Nazi police, came to the house twice. Roger was in fact at that very moment in Switzerland, helping someone to cross the frontier. A telephone call from a friend warned him not to come back right away because if he did he would be in the greatest danger.

When the war ended, he found himself in a completely different situation. German prisoners of war were housed in two camps nearby. They were at great risk from a local population who, at last freed from Germany tyranny, might have been tempted to the same hatred which had made victims of them in the first place. The Community grew against all odds. Visitors increased, among them Catholic priests, pastors of the Reformed churches and many others. These visitors became curious about a religious community which did not seem to belong to any particular tradition. This was one of the reasons that visitors found the life of common prayer so deeply attractive and refreshing.

Roger encountered rigidity when he tried to use the local Roman Catholic church which stood at the heart of the village. Unused for regular worship since the French Revolution, it was opened only for the funeral services of villagers. There was no parish priest and no likelihood of one arriving. This area of Burgundy had a long history of anti-clericalism. The brothers had settled in a place hostile to Christianity. Roger knew this. It appealed to him. The work of reconciliation would have to begin locally. The Community saw this lovely, simple church as the answer to one of their needs. They were becoming more popular and needed a place for prayer. With the permission of the local dean the church was opened up and used for their daily prayers. Suddenly a message came from the relevant authority informing them that permission was withdrawn.

The Community approached the Bishop of Autun, who seemed to be on their side. Although he was very sympathetic to the Community and he knew that the Catholic Church had no plans to use the building, he was reluctant to give them the permission they desired. The view was that it seemed that Catholic churches should be used for Catholic worship only — even if this logic seemed to rule out the possibility of the church being used at all. But Roger and the community knew that they had to press home the point. Courteously but firmly they persisted with their enquiry. In 1948 the Papal Nuncio in Paris extended to them a *simultaneum*. This gave authority for a church building to be used for ecumenical as well as Catholic worship. The Papal Nuncio was in time to become a great friend to the Community. His name was Angelo Roncalli, later Pope John XXIII.

So with great joy on Easter Day 1949, in the little church at Taizé, Roger and six other brothers took their lifelong vows committing themselves to God and one another — to celibacy and community life. The unique feature of this act, largely ignored at the time, was that the Reformed churches in Europe had no experience of monastic communities, and yet some of their members were forming a community. In the Anglican Church the revival of the religious life is over a hundred years old. Here was the remarkable spectacle of Continental Protestants binding themselves together under God in a monastic community. No wonder Taizé puzzled, excited, exasperated and bewildered people at the one and the same time!

Even then it was apparent that Brother Roger's real purpose was not to start a kind of Reformed monasticism parallel to those found in the Catholic and Orthodox traditions. To have done so would have been to create a structure that would have proved to be a barrier against closer links between Christians of different denominations. On the contrary, through a commitment in a life whose roots went back beyond the Reformation, he wished to create what he has called a 'parable of communion'.

Taizé presented problems for Roman Catholic discipline in those pre-Vatican II days. Even though Angelo Roncalli's *simultaneum* allowed that the church could be used for ecumenical worship, the authorities in Rome let it be known that the Catholic Mass could not be celebrated in the church at Taizé now that it was used for the community's worship. The Bishop of Autun was ordered to declare this decision throughout his diocese. In effect it meant that Catholics should steer clear of Taizé. The Bishop was dismayed. He was deeply impressed with the quality of life in the tiny community and could not see Taizé as a threat to true faith. The brothers, though deeply disappointed, were not put off. Through a friend, Cardinal Gerlier, a request was made for Brother Roger to see Pope Pius XII in Rome. Largely as a result of this historic meeting, a change came about in the attitude of the Catholic Church in regard to ecumenism. Local bishops were granted responsibility for deciding whether Catholics within a diocese might take part in ecumenical gatherings. The way was finally opened for Roman Catholics to take part in worship at Taizé in good conscience. They did so in increasing numbers.

Protestants also found Taizé difficult to understand. Roger was well known as a Swiss Protestant. French Protestants naturally then expected him to identify closely with the Reformation tradition. As rumours circulated about the strange new customs developing at Taizé which seemed to align the community more with Rome than Geneva, Protestant leaders converged on Taizé to persuade them into a firmer connection with the Churches of the Reformation. Pastor Marc Boegner, then President of the Federation of Protestant Churches in France, called Roger to Paris for a showdown. Harsh words were said. Pastor Boegner deplored Roger's openness to the Catholic Church. All this was regrettably understandable in the light of the unfortunate history of Catholicism and Protestantism in

France. Roger sought to explain quietly that he had no intention of forsaking the gospel of Jesus Christ. The intention of the Community was to get behind historic divisions to the gospel which unites all Christians, the good news which could reconcile all humanity. The intention of the community was neither to create a new church or sect nor to live solely within one particular tradition of the Church. Its vocation was to be a community of reconciliation. It was to be open to all, Catholics and members of the Reformed churches alike. It was to be a community of hope which embraced all Christians. Thus Taizé would become a parable of communion, a sign of reconciliation which might lead on to the eventual unity of the Church. The brothers were not deluded about the magnitude of their task, but the bold faith which inspired their witness led them to believe that God would give it his blessing.

He did. The Community grew in influence, bringing together leaders of the different traditions for prayer and discussion. Pastor Boegner and his wife became devoted friends of Taizé. So did the Bishop of Autun. Church leaders started to meet at Taizé and found it a place where they were welcome and appreciated. The message of Taizé began to travel everywhere. Visitors came from all directions. By the late 1950s the little church was too small to accommodate all the worshippers. The young were particularly excited by Taizé. It offered a version of the faith which though deeply traditional was deeply radical.

However, the enormous interest in the community from other Christians, particularly the young, alarmed the brothers. How could they cope with this invasion? Roger explained: 'It was never our intention to do anything like this. We intended to be a small group of men bound for life by a commitment to God — a life of prayer, a contemplative life, but we would work to keep ourselves. We had no idea that God had other ideas for us.' The original aim, he told me, was for a community of twelve brothers! Today there are almost 100 Taizé brothers. With pilgrims coming from all over the world, even in the depths of winter numbers rarely fall below hundreds. Indeed from spring to autumn there might be as many as 6,000 in residence at Taizé.

Roger's description of the early years of the Community were interrupted by the sonorous bell calling us all to worship. Later that evening I met with a group of young Anglicans and I asked them what they had found most strange about Taizé. 'Are any of you finding any aspects of life here difficult or objectionable?' I asked. A few from more decidedly Evangelical background put up their hands and said: 'Not exactly difficult but certainly very unusual. We are not used to candles in worship or so much silence and such quiet music.' Others from the Catholic tradition felt worship lacked certain familiar elements — the Hail Mary, ordered processions and a clearer focus upon the priesthood. But everyone was agreed that Taizé did not threaten good traditions but offered a new way forward.

What is the character of this new way?

Later in the evening over a simple meal I was able to ask Roger what he considered to be the way forward for Christian traditions which over the years have become estranged from one another. Roger did not answer the question directly. Instead he returned to the history of Taizé. He remarked that when the Community started the brothers found that the gospels spoke powerfully to their needs and informed their vision. The Beatitudes of Jesus, which he considered to be 'an essential text', especially spoke to them. Three concepts from the Beatitudes seemed to sum up the gospel character of a Christian community — joy, simplicity and mercy.

As I pondered on this later I began to realize that these terms could well apply to the 'strangeness' which so bedevils our links with fellow-Christians. Because we have developed separately, when we encounter one another we seem to meet as strangers. Our traditions, precious and harmless as they may appear to us, may be to others centres of deep doctrinal conflicts and carriers of dark meaning. I recall that in my own Christian pilgrimage as a young man, emerging from an enthusiastic but stark Evangelical Anglican church, Anglo-Catholicism seemed (when I discovered it) to be very strange indeed. The candles, the sign of the cross, the genuflecting, the incense and the formal liturgy — these things were not only mysterious but they felt very divisive. Anglo-Catholicism was so strange that it appeared to be a different gospel. I and others feared it because it did not fit our terms of reference. We dismissed it as incompatible with the gospel we knew. Since those days I have met Anglo-Catholics whose experience have been exactly the same as mine — their exposure to Evangelical Christianity has been no less traumatic. They have found the reverse: the lack of colour and beauty in Evangelical worship and its word-centred liturgy seeming to suggest an idolatry of a different kind.

While it is certainly true that I have developed and changed a great deal since those days without losing anything of real importance from my Evangelical roots, similar prejudices, misunderstandings and fears can be replicated a million times today. How may we reach out to one another with a different attitude and a deeper tenderness?

We need to rediscover the *joy to be found in the diversity*.
There is no single type of person who responds to God. His
Good News can be heard by people of great diversity. This
is a joyful discovery for many people at Taizé. They
encounter the 'strangeness' of finding a common faith with
others with whom no other bond exists. At this level diversity is a gift from God which enlarges our understanding of
his Church. A number of our Anglican young people had
never met Polish, Russian, Spanish or even French
Christians. They found that most of them were Roman
Catholic Christians. One English girl from Liverpool said:
'I've always thought Roman Catholics had a different
religion. Now I know better. I've gained so much through
the love of Christ that such people have taught me here.'
Some of our young people reported that lots of their new
friends had never heard of Anglicanism and that put them
firmly in their place! 'I've always thought that *everyone*
knew about the Church of England!' said one person
incredulously to me. 'And, you know, I had to explain how
we were different from Roman Catholics, on the one hand,
and Methodists on the other.' Taizé got these young people
to look behind their traditions to the joy of the gospel shared
by us all — a joy made all the richer through the discovery
of the diversity of a faith rooted in a common Lord.

But encounter with other Christians may also bring
home the richness of our own Christian experience. At one
of our meals we met a priest from an Orthodox parish in
Moscow. He came to Taizé with his family. He and his
wife had been scientists but gradually they began to see the
futility and barrenness of 'atheistic' science. He made a
journey into faith and became a priest in the Orthodox
Church. It was a privilege to meet Fr Vladimir and his wife
and family. They came to Taizé not only for inspiration for

their spiritual lives but also as a resource for his church. He was hoping to bring ten of his lay people to experience the common prayer and to get a glimpse of how to exercise a renewed ministry as lay Christians. But why do they look to Taizé, to poor little Western Christianity, for inspiration when we in the West so often look to them? It could be that we do not recognize our own gifts and privileges. We have not experienced — at least in the United Kingdom — the harrowing ordeal of persecution which included inability to carry out normal Christian ministries in parishes, hospitals, prisons and other places in society where people congregate or are in need. We take such access for granted. We in the Church of England are blessed by a pastoral ministry which is available to everyone in the land. That is something foreign to experience in Eastern Europe. But now new opportunities are opening up there. The churches of the former Soviet Union are now having confiscated properties returned, with new opportunities to serve their people and lead others to God. They look to the West to assist them in rebuilding their Christian ministry. Taizé is playing a vital part in the reconstruction of the East as it enables people from the former Soviet territories to encounter the best traditions of Western Christianity.

However, the strange encounter with people speaking other languages with whom we seem to have nothing in common can be very disturbing at first. And not everyone who goes to Taizé has a deep or secure faith already. Some people are searching; others simply arrive in a group scarcely knowing what to expect.

I was told that a group of English youths once arrived at Taizé, brought by their vicar. As soon as they got there they asked where the pool tables were! They were unprepared for the rigours of Taizé. They thought that France was exotic but not this strange. They had not expected that they would have to join in the life of a religious community. And they certainly didn't want to help with all the jobs to be done. On their second day they reached an agreement with the brother in charge of the English pilgrims that they would do the bare minimum. With long faces they consented to come to church in the morning and evening and attend their morning group. Within 48 hours they were participating in everything, their attitude completely changed. What was the reason for this extraordinary 'conversion'? They had met a group of Polish girls, all keen Catholics, and so appeared at every teaching session holding hands. They certainly experienced the joy of human diversity — we can only hope that the joy of the gospel was caught as well.

It is certainly true that not all encounters between different cultures and traditions at Taizé go smoothly. One Taizé brother told me that one day a group of Indonesian pilgrims reported that some people were engaging in erotic dancing at the back of Oyak (the café at Taizé). He went to investigate this alarming report. He came across a group of young people from Scotland doing — Scottish dancing! What had scandalized the Indonesians was that the men were holding the women by their waists. To them it was the height of indecency. The brother, thus relieved, was able to interpret one culture to another.

In spite of such troubles as cultures apparently clashing, Taizé reminds us that our joy in the gospel is reflected in our joy in each other as followers of Jesus Christ. Christianity is a corporate religion. The discovery of diversity lies at the heart of finding that the different parts of the body of

Christ enrich the whole.

But we also need to rediscover the *simplicity of worship*. Young Anglicans expressed their appreciation of Taizé worship and contrasted it unfavourably with worship in their parish churches. They complained about how complicated Anglican worship seemed to be. It did not connect with their experience and youth culture. They spoke of hymns and chants which appeared 'boring' and 'difficult'. Sermons and addresses were criticized as being too long, often irrelevant and difficult to understand. Although they realized that Taizé's ways of worship cannot be replicated everywhere, they did point out that it offered a challenge to the forms we possessed. The challenge was not only to consider ways in which the simplicity of faith may come across through liturgy but also to help people discover truths which were commonplace to us.

I asked some of our young people to give me examples of truths they had discovered. One young man from an Evangelical background spoke of using the sign of the cross. One of the brothers had apparently explained that it was originally a 'secret sign' which grew out of persecution in the early Church. For the young man this explanation immediately cut it off from its apparent 'Catholic' tradition and made it possible for him to use devotionally. Another young person had never been helped to understand how she might use an icon or a cross or a picture as an aid in prayer. Another person from a Catholic background found the Bible teaching of Taizé especially helpful. For her the Bible had come alive. She felt she could now appreciate the Evangelical tradition, she remarked.

But worship at Taizé is a lot more elusive than many might think. It does have a simple structure but it is not always immediately understood. Many languages are used in the songs and readings. Nothing is ever announced or explained. The *direction* of worship, however, is simple: it is directed towards God. Some of our young people felt that all their energy at home was directed towards the Alternative Service Book. In too many Anglican churches we offer too many books as people enter church, making the whole offering of worship book-dependent. At Taizé you are *simply* caught up in worship. That's why that terrible word so beloved of young people — 'boring' — seemed never to be used about it.

As I reflected further on what the young people were telling me I realized how powerful was the message of Taizé ecumenically. In bringing people from different traditions together, in providing worship in which 'Catholic' and 'Protestant' could feel equally comfortable and at home, deep seated hostilities were being faced and fears removed. Common worship drawing upon all traditions and cultural backgrounds, anchored in the simplicity of faith, is of profound significance in bringing Christians together.

The third word that Brother Roger had used as one of the foundational words at the heart of the community was 'mercy'. We find the mercy of God in receiving us and that provides the motivation for us *rediscovering the mercy of the gospel in one another*. At Taizé there is an endearing Christian tolerance which I am sure springs from Roger's deep love for all people. It is as if we find on entering Taizé the unspoken message: 'You are greatly loved here for the person you are. We don't expect you to come on our terms but on your own. Be yourself here and make your own journey, without hindrance to the Lord of the Church.'

Another scriptural word closely related to 'mercy' is *kindness*. I was struck by how often this word was used by the brothers. I recall asking one of the young brothers to say how tensions and difficulties were handled by the Community when things went wrong — as they must from time to time. His reply was prompt: 'There is a kindness at the heart of this community. It stems from the humility we all feel at being called by God to serve him. It originates from the fact that we are all weak and vulnerable human beings and in need of mercy ourselves.' As he spoke I remembered that the Greek word for 'kind', *chrestos*, is just one letter away from the word for Christ, *Christos* — a reminder that our behaviour towards one another should reflect his love and kindness for us all.

At Taizé there's a rich awareness of the Church but a deep indifference to any denominationalism that cuts Christian off from Christian. To put it more technically: Christology dominates ecclesiology. Christ comes before the Church — or at least those forms of church life which are based more on human forms of power than the love and kindness we find in Christ.

To return to my conversation with Roger. He took it up where we had left it earlier. Since 1969, he told me, the Community has included many different traditions. There were now brothers from the Reformed, Anglican, Lutheran and Catholic traditions. And since it was quite clear to the brothers that they were not starting a new denomination but responding to a radical vocation to reconciliation at all levels, support for the different Christian churches became a marked feature of the community. Many a person disillusioned by the life of their home church has been given fresh encouragement through the help of the brothers. Brother Roger was willing to share his own story with me: 'Without becoming a symbol of repudiation for anyone at all, following my grandmother's example, I discovered my

Christian identity in reconciling within myself the current of faith of my Protestant background with the faith of the Catholic Church.'

Three

....

Journey into self and community

The distinctive thing about Taizé is the Community itself. There is no sense of hierarchy and even leadership is a shared charge as the brothers take responsibility together for the life of the community. Brother Roger's place in this is of course crucial but not in the usual style of leadership. He is not so much head of the Community as at the heart of it. While all the time reference is made to him, you will find him deferring to others as much as they defer to him. There is mutual listening, sharing and respect. The individual submits to the Community and the Community listens attentively to each individual.

It is often forgotten that we can only find ourselves in relation to others. This fact became a reality for one of our English pilgrims when she was at Taizé. Mary remarked that she had always got on well with others but had never thought about the connection between herself and other people until this experience. Taizé shook her deeply. She was impressed by the quality of community life and the way the brothers cared for one another. Self was sublimated in the interests of others. It showed in simple ways: the courtesy of the community for all in need; the calm approach to organizing the site even with 6,000 people there. Above all, it showed in Brother Roger's attitude to his young brothers. She noticed, as I did, that as Roger entered the church he would gently touch a brother's shoulder as he passed. It was almost as if he was saying 'I am aware of you. Thank you for being you.'

'Touching' is an apt description of the impact of the Christian faith. We begin the Christian life with God's touch at baptism. In the rite, the reading from Scripture often used recalls the occasion when Jesus took children in his arms and blessed them. Whether our pilgrimage began with baptism when we were children or adults, we were taken into the arms of Christ and blessed. He touched us with his love. In the early Church the anointing with oil was considered to be a 'sealing' in which the Holy Spirit touched the believer with his grace, making the Christian the repository of the Spirit.

Christian community begins and ends with the touch of God on our lives. It is he who creates community. There can be no Christian community which does not have as its centre the life of God. At Taizé, Brother Roger is distinctly uncomfortable if any see him as director and guru of the Community. He shies away from adulation of any kind. He refuses the traditional monastic term 'superior' for his role. He is content to be called 'brother' to describe his position within the Community. For him and his fellows God the Trinity is the pattern of Christian life, where there is no distinction of status despite the distinctiveness of persons bound in love to one another.

At one of the evening meals sitting under the trees looking over the open plain below I opened a discussion with the brothers about the relationship between our individual identities and the communities to which we belong. 'Why is it', I asked, 'that our communities can be for some the cause of great blessing and growth but for others the reason for personal damage and psychological hurt? How is it that communities can make us and break us? What lessons has Taizé for other Christian fellowships?'

Brother Roger's reply was to remind us all of the primary fact of community. Community does not begin when we decide to accept the Christian faith and join the Church. The Christian community is already in existence and ready for us, just as a family is ready for us when we are born. Just as it is ridiculous for a child to say 'I created community when I was born', so it is to regard ourselves as creators of community or centres of it. In Roger's estimate that realization is the start of humility. God is always there before us. He is the necessary condition for community. We are but accidental. But this does not mean that we are unimportant. God regards every person as precious and unique. Because he sets his love upon each one of us we matter to God's community and our contribution is consequently vital. We have the power to make or break community life.

As Roger spoke of the nature of community I saw him as a powerful symbol of the coming together of two great traditions in the Church — Evangelical and Catholic — in the communion of the Spirit. In Christian history these traditions have not always been allies — indeed, they have been bitter enemies at times. Taizé has been remarkable in bringing both together. Brother Roger's role in this has of course been pivotal. He came from a Swiss Evangelical tradition and an element of it is retained in the way he speaks of faith. Although he is not trapped by rigid theories

47

of conversion, he talks with ease of people finding God, knowing God and walking with God. His language is that of the lover who cannot but speak of his beloved in terms of endearment. Brother Roger has never lost that natural and simple faith that made him a follower many years ago. It is in total balance with a profound sense of the complexities of following Christ in a difficult and dangerous world.

But in him too there is a basic Catholicism. He cannot contemplate a Christian all alone, separated from community and from God's grace through other people. Individual discipleship can only be expressed corporately: the very meaning of that word 'corporate' — belonging to the body — takes us back to the notion of 'touch' as fundamental to Christian life. The touch on the shoulder as worship begins is a physical sign of a spiritual reality. We belong to a God who has touched us in body, mind and spirit.

I pressed home some questions about living in community. 'What are the sticking points? How does one handle problems of tiredness, envy, irritability and even sexuality? Does anybody ever challenge the rules — and if so, on what grounds?'

Laughter punctuated the questions I posed and several of the young brothers vigorously intervened to put me right. They readily acknowledged that Taizé was not a perfect community. Community had to be worked at, individuals had to learn to tolerate one another and to become aware of the strengths and weakness of others. One brother spoke of the importance of apologizing whenever we step out of line. Another mentioned that problems of tiredness and irritability were readily acknowledged as human weaknesses which can destroy community. Understanding of factors which create these conditions was viewed as essential in order to eradicate them. Once again, the bell calling us to worship cut short an enjoyable discussion.

It was a pity that the conversation ended at that point because I am sceptical that any community or family can exist without conflict. And I'm suspicious of claims that moral determination alone can eradicate conflict. At Taizé, though, we have to acknowledge a unity of vision and purpose which means that conflicts seem transient. How, I wondered, does this relate to Brother Roger's own personality? He may eschew the term 'superior' but he is the focus of the Community's life. He presides like a venerable father over every meal, sharing his thoughts with his brothers and introducing his guests. The Community is bound together not least in loyalty to him. He may claim to be no more than 'a poor servant of communion' in a community already blessed by God, but his gentle spirit pervades the whole of Taizé.

It was Herbert Kelly, the founder of the Society of the Sacred Mission (the Kelham Fathers), who once said that religious communities in the Church of England should not outlive the memory of their founder. He believed there should always be a new vision for a new age, and the temptation in the religious life to hold on to a vision from the past needed to be avoided at all costs.

I have no idea what plans have been made at Taizé for community life after Brother Roger. But what impressed me was a remarkable openness to the future. So many conflicts in family, community and church life are caused by a desire to hold on to some heritage from the past. The apparently minimal conflicts at Taizé may be due to the way the Community travels light, seeking not to pre-serve but to serve. If I am right, it's yet another lesson from Taizé for all Christian churches.

Further reflection on the nature of community and the

individual's place in it led me to go to three key words that are crucial to our common life together — love, submission and holiness.

'Love', someone once said, 'is not the opposite of hate but of selfishness.' One of the young pilgrims said later in the week that the one thing that made all the difference to him at Taizé was the realization that he was loved by God. Because he was loved, he felt released to share that love with others. Being loved by God leads to a generous, loving approach to others. God's love is not for us to receive in isolation from others and to be hogged for ourselves. It makes us more loving.

This reflection led me to remember a personal event when I was Principal of Trinity College, Bristol, some years ago. One particular colleague was vocal in his opposition to some of the proposed changes. It was my responsibility to deal with this difficult man. As I walked towards my study for the appointment which was likely to be confrontational, my mind was set on battle. I then became disturbed. A battle! With whom? My enemy? Surely not. He was a fellow-Christian and colleague — just as committed as I was to the future of the college. Our differences were not of kind but of degree. We both loved God and wanted to serve him. Our differences arose out of a deep loyalty to the God we worshipped and the college we served. We differed simply in our perceptions of the problems and possible solutions.

As I walked up the hill to the college, my attitude began to change. I saw my colleague as a brother in Christ, as someone who needed my support, not my antagonism; my love and not my anger. As a result the meeting was transformed by my approach to my friend. I could sense his tenseness as we sat down. I began by thanking him for his rich contribution to the college and I apologized if I had misunderstood his point of view. I went on to say that the time had come for us to share deeply our concerns for the college and what resolutions we might have. As I introduced the matter in this way I felt the tension go from my body and as I glanced across to him I saw his face softening too.

The upshot was a deepened friendship, a frank sharing of painful issues that divided us and a ready acceptance to work at the problems together. I shall never forget the lesson I learned that morning, which was essentially to see him as a dear friend and one greatly loved by God. As we shook hands that morning it was the affectionate touching of friendship. Our relationship had been transformed by my change of attitude. In a way, only I as Principal and therefore the senior staff member could have made that possible. I had to give love.

It is that kind of acceptance of one another and love for each other that strikes people when they visit Taizé. It is often the case that when one goes away on youth camps or Christian conferences the expectation for the visitor to 'behave', 'conform' or 'keep to the rules' is signalled strongly. Such expectations may place an unwarranted burden on people or may work against the spirit of 'grace' which every Christian community wishes to impart. Taizé is remarkably free of 'rules'; indeed, it provides a basic freedom which enables young people to relax and feel at home. There is no pressure to conform to what other people want or expect.

The second word that I meditated upon at Taizé was *submission*. A number of our English young people were impressed by the way that the brothers listened to one another, regarded others as their equals and sought to live an egalitarian life. 'It contrasts', a girl observed, 'with the hierarchical life we have in our society back home.' Yes, I echoed mentally, it clashes too with the hierarchical life in the Church throughout the world. Somehow we need to 'pay attention to others' in the way that this Community does. However, hierarchy by itself is not the problem. The Bible and the Christian tradition generally accepts the fact that within any community there will be those who will have leadership, who will exercise authority and discipline. Brother Roger may only be the first among equals but he is the undoubted leader of the Community. The New Testament tells us that we all have a responsibility to 'esteem very highly those set over you in the Lord'. In this world which is eager to emphasize equality and egalitarianism, the note of obedience strikes us all as a most unfashionable word. We find ourselves apologizing for it these days. We should not do so: obedience is a requirement that emerges from our discipleship as Christians. Of course, some will say 'Well, we expect Archbishops to go on about authority because they want to get their own way!' Well, I know I leave myself open to that criticism. Unrepentantly, I press home the point. To be a Christian is to be 'under obedience' to those over us in the Church. If we deny this our discipleship becomes irresponsible and individualistic.

This in turn demands a double responsibility. First, from those of us who have authority in community or church life: the authority entrusted to us is a service which we must exercise for those set under us. We have to cherish those whose ministries we can influence and, in some cases, affect for good or ill. Authority can be a dangerous weapon in the wrong hands. The pattern before all leaders is the One who reckoned himself a servant of others. We shall not go far wrong in our discipleship if we keep before us the words of the Lord who said in one of his parables: 'When you have done all you have been commanded to do, say "We are unworthy servants; we have only done our duty".'

Of course, we have to recognize that sometimes abuses of authority stem from the reaction of those who are not secure in the authority entrusted to them. They may feel unworthy of it or threatened by others around them. This may lead them to retaliate defensively or to hug the trappings of authority tightly around them, in order to feel secure. The security of insecurity. This all too familiar situation will demand from those assisting such a threatened leader considerable sensitivity and gentleness as they seek to help the one who is having such a crisis of roles.

The other side of the coin is the situation confronting those who serve under others. It takes as much grace to be led as to lead. The lowliness to accept the authority of others is as demanding as the loneliness of leadership. Those who have particular gifts to offer may well be frustrated when their gifts are ignored or overlooked.

Common to both situations is the often ignored fact of 'power': power to influence others, to control and manipulate. This exists even in the most Christian and religious community as well as in the most secular business company. Whereas in the latter the fact of power is explicitly recognized and accepted as part of the structure of a business community, in a religious community the presence of power may be overlooked. We may pride ourselves on our communal fellowship and love, and state that 'worldly' structures of authority have no place here. This is the road to a denial of realities which may lead to demonic powers over others. We can take as an extreme example of this the terrible events at Waco in Texas when the power of a 'charismatic' but unbalanced individual led to violence and death. Such manipulation of power is of course rare. But power over people is present in all communities and may be used for beneficial or evil ends. In all groups decisions have to be made and leadership has to be exercised. The question is: how is power to be exercised so that it builds up the community and does not lead to polarization and division?

One answer has already been given — that of love. Love is radical in its acceptance of others and their worth. A leader who loves others will listen to the community and this will guide the exercise of leadership. A leader who loves others will submit himself to the needs of the community and will heed advice which flows from others. It was 'submission' that our young people noted in Brother Roger at Taizé: his willingness to listen and learn even from the most junior and newest brother in the community, even from the newest arrival amongst the pilgrims at Taizé.

One of my questions about life in the community did not get an answer because we ran out of time. It is necessary to raise it in this book because it is so important, so troublesome and so delicate. It is the subject of our sexuality and the moral questions that surround the whole area of sex. It is something which may either separate communities or enrich them: it may destroy individuals or strengthen their effectiveness.

Sadly, often the attitude of the Church to sex has been far from wholesome and positive. At times in history sex has been regarded as shameful and embarrassing. Women have been feared as having seductive powers to pull men away from the paths of holiness. This has diminished women as well as men. The positive aspects of God's gift of our sexuality have often been overlooked, much to our loss.

Over the last twenty years a sexual revolution has taken place which has affected all of us more than we realize. It is rare these days to encounter people who think of our sexual desires as a 'predicament' or a 'problem'. These are more likely to be regarded as natural functions which should be enjoyed and directed towards personal fulfilment. The pendulum has swung to the other extreme. To have sex and to enjoy it seems elevated almost to a human right. Indeed, anyone who is not sexually active is viewed with a certain amount of incredulity or disdain. As long as a sexual relationship does not hurt another person, it can't be wrong.

The control we now possess over human reproduction has further encouraged this view. Women need not fear an unwanted pregnancy. All that is required is control of the situation. It is only sex without precautions which is regarded as foolish. Such then is the sexual revolution which is the backdrop against which young people have to work out the meaning of their lives and the nature of their relationships.

Their difficulty may be illustrated by the spread of AIDS, which has only slightly dented the cult of sexual freedom. The scourge of AIDS has, for many, led not to a moral reassessment of their actions, but to an ever more vigorous search for better methods of protection during intercourse. Against this background young people, at school and university, are encouraged in our culture to consider sexual activity a matter more of taste than of morality. Little wonder that so many young Christians are confused concerning the matter and in need of guidance. What guidelines come from the Christian faith to help us in our search for a positive approach to our multi-faceted sexuality?

The search has to be set in the context of our nature as human beings. We are not beings who simply *happen* to be sexual creatures: we *are* sexual creatures. We are created male and female. Furthermore, God himself created us like this and it was his will. It was part of his good plan for our lives that we should find each other attractive and that sexual intercourse should be so fulfilling. Nevertheless, the story of creation is followed by the Fall. Our sexuality has been distorted by the sin as much as any other part of our humanity. That means to say that selfishness and self-aggrandizement have come to dominate our sexual instincts quite as much as other aspects of our lives. The truth that these are God-given does not militate against the fact that if they are used wrongly they have the power to destroy. Like fire, sex can be very wonderful in the right context — and very destructive in the wrong.

So how can we ensure that these instincts are, to quote the Prayer Book, 'hallowed and directed aright'? There are two messages which it is vital to communicate to this and every generation.

First, we should encourage our young people to see sexual intercourse in the context of the marriage relation-ship. It is designed to be the physical expression of the deepest of all human commitments one to another. The giving of oneself to another or, as the marriage service in the Alternative Service Book puts it, 'to know one another in love', is among God's richest gifts. When we separate intercourse from a permanent and faithful relationship earthed in love, friendship and respect, we are reducing it to much less than it was intended to be.

Second, and following on from this, if we are to take God's guidance seriously then it will require considerable self-discipline. That is another unfashionable idea. In some

Daily prayer (© Ateliers et Presses de Taizé)

A group discussion (© William Clemmey)

The queue at Oyak (© William Clemmey)

Informal talk (© William Clemmey)

circles it is taken for granted that it is impossible for people to abstain from sexual intercourse. The Christian ideal that we should abstain from it until marriage is shrugged aside as difficult and unnecessary. But we need not follow our culture by regarding sex as an impulse that *must* be gratified. To do so is to deprive us of an important aspect of our human dignity, as creatures who have the capacity for choice. Our sexual desires can be controlled just as we control any other aspect of our make-up. To suggest other-wise would be to say that our instincts cannot come under the control of our minds and morals.

However, it would be foolish in the extreme to deny the fact that our sexual drives are a formidable force in human experience. None of us can cast a stone at others. It is no surprise that at times we find ourselves doing things which, in the light of God's love, we have cause to regret. But as we seek to exercise self-discipline God does not leave us to strive on our own. Christians do have the power of God upon whom they can draw. God's Holy Spirit can and does give us the power to live holy lives for him.

This leads on to a third word I meditated upon at Taizé — *holiness*. Holiness is a rich word meaning far more than abstaining from something, which is usually the nuance we place on the word. It means 'to set apart something for God'. To make holy means to dedicate something or some-one to God's service. When a person decides to follow Christ he or she decides to live the kind of life that God wants: a holy life. It does not mean that the person is perfect. It does mean that he or she is under new manage-ment and striving to please God. Furthermore, holiness depends for its strength on the power and grace of God through the Holy Spirit. We are all aware of how weak and sinful we are. Christianity is not a religion that depends on what we do but on what God has already done for us in Christ. His resources are available for us here and now.

And all this takes me back to Taizé and its community. I never did get the opportunity to discuss some of these delicate matters in depth with the brothers but some of the answers are transparently clear. Holiness is central to Taizé. For Brother Roger, the fact that the brothers choose to be single (celibate) is not a statement that marriage is inferior but that for some people God offers another way to serve him. For the Taizé brothers, the way of celibacy is their offering to our Lord. It is not a denial of human love but the giving of oneself to our Lord so that the brothers may give themselves more fully to others. In one of his letters Brother Roger writes: 'Christ alone can convert our passions into total love of our neighbours . . . there is no love for our neighbour without the cross. Only by the Cross can we know the unfathomable depths of love.'

And Taizé encourages people to give themselves to others. This was the experience of my fellow bishop, Peter Nott, at Taizé. Peter told me of an amazing thing that happened to him:

> I arrived a few days before you to prepare for the arrival of the party. I was standing outside the church when a young man detached himself from a group that was leaving Taizé, and ran to me smiling broadly. He was a priest, dressed in a black shirt. He was thin and gaunt, his shirt was frayed at the collar and the cuffs, his trousers baggy and greatly patched, his shoes old and cracked. He was clearly a poor man. He walked up to me, smiled and, grasping my hand, kissed my bishop's ring, which is a customary sign of loyalty and love in some churches.

I had no idea what nationality he was or whether he spoke English so I pointed to myself and said 'English'. 'Ah', he smiled and, pointing to himself, said 'Ukraine, from Ukraine'. Then he said 'I have a present for you'. From his pocket he brought a wooden egg, beautifully handpainted. He pressed it into my hand and smiling once more ran to join his fellow pilgrims on his coach.

I walked into the church and held the egg in my hands throughout the Eucharist and felt very close to that young man. I was deeply moved that this young priest from a poor and troubled country had given a gift to a bishop from a rich church and rich country. There was nothing I could give him in return. I had no time to thank him properly and I don't suppose we shall ever meet again until we meet in heaven. And then perhaps I will be able to tell him that his gift, his little kindness, is something I will remember to the end of my life, and his painted egg, which is in my chapel where I see it every day, is one of the most precious gifts I have ever received.

When I read Bishop Peter's moving letter it seemed to me a wonderful illustration of what community is all about. The 'egg' represents all you and I have to offer. Our gifts and abilities, our love and our desires. When we give our 'egg' joyfully and unreservedly God has that gracious capacity to use it to draw someone close to him. The tantalizing thing, of course, is that, as in Bishop Peter's story, we may never know how that 'egg' will be received by the person we give it to and what difference it will make. Perhaps that young priest will read this book and discover that his exuberant act of giving gave an English bishop not only much pleasure but inspired him to see it in an act of love that is 'Calvary-like' in its nature. Oh, if only all our giving to one another took that shape!

Four

....

Journey into stillness and simplicity

'Western Christianity is very noisy', said a young man from the north of England to me during one of our Taizé discussions. He had just been comparing worship in his local church with the worship of Taizé. I asked him to enlarge on his statement. He drew attention to the undeniable fact that there are very few gaps for quietness and reflection in most services in the Church of England. Each moment is filled with activity, almost as if we believe that God will call us to account for every minute of wasted time. Other young people agreed. Example after example tumbled out of wordy services. They were not talking about charismatic worship but about the straightforward Anglican diet. Long lessons, lots of prayers, dull sermons, hymns that dragged on and on. They complained that it occupied the mind without releasing the spirit. By contrast, they admired the simplicity of Taizé worship and the breathtaking silence that would descend upon 5,000 people in prayer. As they spoke I recalled E.M. Forster's great novel *A Passage to India* where one of the characters compares Western Christianity unfavourably with Indian religions, mocking 'poor, little talkative Christianity'.

And yet this indictment is puzzling when one recalls that individual and corporate silence has been a powerful tradition in Christianity from the beginning. Our Lord spent considerable periods of time away from others in the wilderness. He knew how important it was to be still before his Father and in silence to unite the pain of the world with the love of God. Monastic spirituality is based on Christ's example. The Desert Fathers lived in both communal and individual silence. Later on the Quakers were the first Protestant group to encourage corporate silence as a normative element in worship. Yet, somehow, silence has scarcely touched the Church of England at large, especially our public services. The Alternative Service Book is littered with good intentions. Its permissive rubric 'Silence may be kept' invites a response but it is rarely taken up. And when it is, it is usually a cursory twenty seconds. Long enough, perhaps, for people to think that the celebrant has forgotten his place but not long enough for anyone to go deeply into personal prayer and private devotion.

This subject became a topic of conversation with Brother Roger and some of his community. Roger saw the purpose of Taizé as enabling people to meet God. 'For that to happen', he said, 'there must be space to listen to him and space to talk with him. Silence has no particular virtue in itself: it is a means to an end. It is to enable God to break the silence in us.'

Listening. Our modern world finds listening relatively easy to talk about but very hard to put into practice. Take our childhood experiences. Most of us can remember parents and teachers telling us to listen to adults. We were instructed to 'pay attention' to them and we may recall being told off severely when we spoke 'before we were spoken to'. But while the well-meaning intentions of such instructions may have been to make us good listeners, in reality the message coming through was that the essence of education was the art of talking. Communication was the name of the game, and those who were regarded as successful were those who could get their point across as powerfully as possible.

So this unspoken but loud assertion follows us through life. Sooner or later, though, the longing for silence makes itself felt in our noisy, competitive world. But by then our ability to hear the deeper music of the spirit may have already been affected adversely by the deafening roar of the world. Like some people deafened prematurely by shell-shock or the ear-piercing cacophony of ghetto-blasters, we may become unable to listen to the rich tones of our inner life or the even more profound melodies of the Spirit of God.

The experience of many at Taizé is that bad habits can be unlearned: the spiritually deaf can hear again. True, stillness is easier at a place like Taizé than in our offices, shops, factories and homes. Brother Roger did not deny this, but he regards Taizé and other religious communities as assisting young people to find God in quietness and in one another through worship and through the loving support of fellow-Christians from around the world.

Oddly, Taizé really is a place of many words. There are hosts of groups: there are countless conversations over meals, there are lots of debates and discussions at Oyak (the café and the only place at Taizé where alcohol may be bought and consumed, though carefully rationed). Laughter is there in abundance, and transcends the language barriers. There are many talks given by the brothers; there is a weekly address given by Brother Roger himself. But Taizé is unlike any Christian assembly or conference any of us is likely to attend: it is not a didactic community which tries to influence people by the power of rhetoric. The words used in worship are few and often repeated. One simple song may be repeated twenty times and last eight minutes. This may well be followed by a great silence making us aware of stillness all around. In this respect Taizé is a place of few words. The quiet embrace of God enfolds you as the words grow less. Taizé makes it possible for busy people to encounter silence and stillness. In some cases it is for the first time in their lives. It is often a transforming experience, an experience which may last a lifetime.

But like other great experiences it has to be worked at continually. The question remains: How can any of us with normal work and family responsibilities make enough room for silence?

During my time at Taizé I meditated on Psalm 46. The psalm reflects Israel's experience of waiting on God at a time when everything around appeared to be crumbling. It begins with a bold and courageous statement of faith: 'The Lord of hosts is with us; the God of Jacob is our refuge.' The context of this great affirmation of God's presence soon becomes apparent. The people of God were threatened on every side. The writer draws upon three images: natural disaster, political unrest and military action. The psalm proclaims: We shall not fear – *even though*

(1)   the earth should change and the mountains shake in the heart of the sea (verse 2);

(2)   the nations rage and kingdoms totter (verse 6);

(3)   wars, bows, spears and chariots threaten the people of God (verse 9).

This psalm came alive for me at Taizé. It seemed to speak of our own age. We live in a violent world in which everything appears to be shaken or questioned. Even those who believe in God find themselves worrying about a disintegrating society. And we are as dismayed by natural disasters as any previous generation.

But then I began to see that though the imagery of the psalm is violent, violence itself is not its subject. God is the subject. No matter how gloomy the prospect or how dire the future may seem, nothing can diminish the power of God's presence:

> The Lord of hosts is with us;
> The God of Jacob is our refuge.

This refrain is the heartbeat of the psalm, repeated after the three parts in which the violence of nature, political activity and military action threaten the city of God.

But what is this city? The psalm talks about the presence of God with us. How are we to discern him? The city of God is found dwelling within the world, giving it meaning and value: 'There is a river whose streams make glad the city of God, the holy habitation of the Most High. God is in the midst of her, she shall not be moved; God will help her right early.'

The imagery of a river constantly flowing and nourishing the city speaks of the permanence of God with us. This city is not a blueprint for an indefinite future but a statement of fact. The city is here already; it exists here and now. God is not an occasional traveller who pays a visit if he feels like it. He lives amongst us.

When a Christian reads this psalm the incarnation comes to mind. The Lord of hosts lives amongst us, and he has shown this to be so in Christ our Lord. Jesus not only lived but died amongst us. His passion and death are referred to as the *work of Christ*. So when the psalm says 'Come, behold the works of the Lord' we think of the work of Christ, where God met the violence of the world head on, and overcame it by dying for us and rising from death to put hope in us.

But at Taizé I also considered carefully the fact that in our world where there is such unbelief there is also such fear. It is a striking fact that over my thirty years of ministry when I have got very close to professional and successful people they have confided in me their terror of death. Life seems so impermanent to them that they dread the time when they will be no more. They have been so successful that they find it unbearable to contemplate that life could go on without them. They value human love so much that they cannot abide the thought that death will part them from their loved ones for ever.

Such fears are very understandable. We have all experienced them and will continue to do so. It is natural to know terror and dread when awful things happen — as they will, to Christians as to anyone. But 'the Lord of hosts is with us'. For followers of Jesus Christ death, disease and disappointment will not have the last word in our lives. Christ has overcome death. 'He is risen' is the eternal gospel proclamation. That is the confident message of our faith. His resurrection is our Magna Carta of life with God for evermore. Christianity is not founded on a lie but on the reality of Christ who is the Truth. We can only cope with fear as we embrace the One who is ever present with us.

Come, behold the works of the Lord. As well as reminding us of the incarnation, the command prompts us to look at what

God is doing in our world today.

And what do we see? If we are unable to look beyond the headlines in the newspapers with their frequent bad news, or beyond the brash lights of our cities or beyond the clamour of advertisers claiming great things for their goods, we will never 'behold the works of the Lord'. There is so much claiming our attention that we are liable to take much for granted — the beauty of nature; its colour and life; the rich diversity and splendour of humanity. Only when we see beyond the immediate do we glimpse the miracle of life itself and the complexity of creation. We sense the miracle of our existence — why is there something rather than nothing, and why 'me'? And our attention switches to the people around us. We think of our families, friends and those we love. From where comes the affection we have for them and they for us? 'Come, behold.' That's all we are asked to do. Those who behold, also marvel. To marvel is not necessarily to seek for explanation. It leads from contemplation to praise and on to a deeper trust. We live in a world which has lost the art of wondering. The effect of secularism is that many people simply assume that this life is all and that nothing is of permanent value. When people start to dig below the surface of 'what is' they usually begin to doubt their unbelief. 'Come, behold . . .'

We also see that 'he makes wars to cease to the ends of the earth; he breaks the bow and shatters the spear in sunder'. We may well question this. Isn't it a fact that wars have not ceased? Indeed, we have 'advanced' from the primitive bow and arrow to much more sophisticated weapons of destruction. Yes, true, but the Psalmist is not saying that peace is a reality. The psalm is set in the context of war. What the Psalmist says is that it is the will of God to bring about disarmament. The psalms are often radical. Psalm 46 makes it clear that violence never works. The history of violence is a history of failure. No war has ever been fought in which even those fighting for righteousness have not had to face the consequences of their own destruction of human life. The fight against Fascism in the Second World War was a righteous cause: Hitler's ideology was inhuman and led to unspeakable horrors. Furthermore, the freedom of the world depended upon good people taking up arms against it. But the very fact of war meant that the allies also destroyed the lives of innocent civilians in their fight against the evils of Nazism. Force is a blunt instrument which may injure the innocent along with the guilty, the citizen as much as the military. It is God's will to do away with violence and bring about the city of God in which a river of peace runs and in which goodness, justice and love meet together.

This kind of contemplation is never simply a wistful hope. Such praying leads irreversibly to action. The God who breaks the spear in sunder does it through his servants like you and me. Prayer is not a religious compensation for social and political action. Prayer is the soil in which righteous action germinates. Sleeves are rolled up when the prayer ends. Strictly speaking, of course, prayer never ends. It directs the course of action.

Be still and know that I am God. The second command in Psalm 46 is to 'be still and know'. Be still. What does it mean to be still? The Hebrew text conveys the idea of 'letting be'. Let God have his way. It is rather like a parent telling a fretful child 'Calm down! It's all right; don't worry. I'm here with you.' The image evokes the picture of Christ in the boat with his fearful disciples and commanding the raging storm by saying 'Be still'. *Be still* is a word to our busy lives; it is a command to take our attention off ourselves and the noise of our world and give God attention. We know from experience that when we are frantic with worry and rushing from here to there we are often incapable of listening. 'Be still' directs us to stop and take in. And this is what Taizé provides for so many. Although at Taizé hundreds of people are moving from place to place, there is a sense of peace and unhurried purpose. And at the centre of the community is the large barn-like church which is never empty. Go into it any time of the day and night and people will be found praying, silently meditating and being still in the presence of God.

In a world where we are bombarded with words Taizé seeks to suppress unnecessary words in worship. Here once more is the attraction of great simplicity. When Scripture is read, you find it is only a few verses. The deliberate intention is to present a few key texts and ideas and to get people to focus on them and live them. Brother Roger's great desire is that all should hear God speaking his Word into our hearts so that his word may dwell richly in us, becoming flesh, lived out in the parable of community. A life of radical simplicity.

Taizé's great desire that it should be a place where God's living Word may speak to all may be illustrated by Brother Roger's way of addressing everyone on the hill at a given time. This happens once a week and we noticed that he never stands to speak. He sits, microphone in hand, talking to thousands as if he was talking to a few friends gathered in his room. He talks with his gentle voice reaching our hearts, speaking to the child of God in each of us, calling and pleading with us to listen. No wonder he is so often surrounded by children who feel that they have a special affinity with him.

But how do busy modern people find space in their diaries for stillness? How may the spirituality of Taizé be adapted to life in the world?

It is often said that modern people have no opportunity for silence. Yet we fill the quiet times in our lives with noise. The temptation when we enter a quiet house is to put on the television or radio. When we get into our cars our instinct is often to put a tape into the stereo, instead of taking advantage of a rare chance to be away from people. There are even those who jog with a Walkman around their waist. It is as if we are frightened to be alone with ourselves before God. Perhaps one of the things which Taizé teaches us is to use creatively and imaginatively the spaces which already exist in our lives. If we looked for those moments today we might find to our surprise and pleasure that there are opportunities for that quiet time with God. Centuries ago a Syrian monk used to urge novice monks to 'put your mind into your heart and stand in the presence of God'. That's good advice. It does require conscious effort but through experience we shall find that the journey from mind to heart will get easier and easier.

And know that I am God. But being still is not enough. In our world there are those who, realizing the need for stillness, seek to find answers in adapting forms of spirituality to be found in other religions. It might be Yoga or other forms of contemplation. Sometimes people invent their own spirituality. I am sure that such things can sometimes be of value to them. Christians have no need to sneer at the journey within undertaken by those who have neither heard nor responded to the gospel. But the 'journey within' requires a focus. And it needs to be something other than simply our own inner self. The journey within is undertaken in the company of the One who is within and without, God himself. 'Be still and *know* that I am God.' The word 'know' smacks of intimacy, of being in a relationship with someone who is valued. In the Old Testament the verb 'to know' is used of sexual intimacy. It describes the way a loving couple express their desire physically for one other. Here in this verse that strong verb is a profound analogy for the vulnerable and deep encounter we can have with Almighty God. Yet how can we 'know' God when he is ultimately beyond our human comprehension?

It is true that God lies beyond the reach of our minds in the same way that the universe, his creation, lies beyond the range of any single telescope. But 'knowing' God is not an intellectual act, even though it is rational. It is not an emotional act, even though it touches the emotions. It is a spiritual act which touches our very being. For us as Christians God has been revealed in Jesus Christ. He is the human face of God. Taizé, as I have already said, is deeply Christ-centred. Prayer and praise are focused on him. His words and actions come through the liturgy and through the chants and songs.

We *know* that even though God is ultimately mysterious we can call him Father because his Son, Jesus, has made God accessible to us. For an American friend it took an operation to make her aware of the closeness of God. Anne Moody is in the media and a few years ago had the frightening experience of breast cancer. She wrote this letter to me.

> It was your statement that God is a *person* that spoke to me. No one had ever suggested such a notion to me before. All of a sudden I could talk to him as I would to anyone. And I did. And he spoke to me for the first time. It was during my year

and a half of cancer treatment, surgeries and hospitalizations. And God showed up in the strangest places. For example, I *knew* He was in the radiation room with me and that He was smiling! Once we even laughed together. Strange place for 'conversion' but it's true.

To return to the passage, the Psalmist is urging his readers to trust God even when the situation seems to be beyond remedy. 'Let God be God', he appears to be insisting. The great French writer and critic of American culture in the last century, De Tocqueville, once remarked of Americans that 'each citizen is habitually engaged in the contemplation of a very puny object, namely himself'. The observation could equally be made of each one of us. We know only too well that we place ourselves at the centre of the universe. Christianity challenges us to shift the focus of worship from ourselves to God, to contemplate his glory, beauty and love.

But this does not result in withdrawal from the world. It is mistaken to assume that places like Taizé or the activity of prayer, whose fruit is stillness and meditation, lead to retreat from the problems of life. True spirituality results in confrontation with hard issues, not denial of them. In this chapter we have considered prayer from within the reality of a violent world and from the viewpoint of Psalm 46. We have seen the Psalmist's 'down to earth' approach. Faith is anchored in the world of suffering and death. The same realism is seen at Taizé. I was struck by Brother Roger's grasp of world issues and the way that the Community kept an eye on what was happening around the globe. They were alert to world events, assessing them with the eye of faith and quick to turn human need into prayer — and then prayer into action. I was reminded constantly that Taizé is an incarnational community seeking to relate faith to the world we live in.

I was equally impressed by the Community's commitment to the world's needs. Living in the village were a group of Bosnian refugees brought to Burgundy by the Community to be in a safe place. Wherever there is violence and suffering the Community seeks ways to be involved. Small communities of Taizé brothers live in places of great spiritual and material need around the world. Worship and prayer leads naturally to service, whether in Burgundy, Bangladesh or Brazil. If prayer is real, you cannot pray for someone or something without it leading to action.

The example set by the brothers is one urged on all Taizé pilgrims. From the Burgundian hillside we must return to the places where broken relationships, violence of speech as well as action and deep anger caused by unemployment and social neglect are facts of daily experience. True prayer does not falter from being exposed to impossible odds because it is rooted in the Lord of Hosts who is with us — who is our refuge always.

SIMPLICITY

Central to our understanding of Psalm 46 is impermanence. The writer sees the world as a changing place where only God, the Lord of hosts, remains the same. The river flows through a city which is at peace with itself because God is in the midst of her. Everything is in flux except the God of the city who is the source of eternal hope and strength to his people.

Taizé is an illustration of this principle. It seems as if it has just been established instead of being a place of pilgrimage and spiritual nourishment for fifty years. At the beginning of Chapter 2, I spoke of the ramshackle impression Taizé makes upon the visitor when he or she arrives. The tents, the dormitories, the huts for meetings — none of them give you a sense of permanence. Seen from outside, the church does not make one's heart leap with aesthetic delight. It is functional, that is all. Taizé is deliberately simple and it has managed to retain a tasteful simplicity by its devotion to impermanence. I was constantly reminded that 'here we have no abiding city — but we seek the one to come'. The message of Taizé is that pilgrimage is the very character of the Christian life.

And Brother Roger emphasized this point again and again. Not for him and his community a lavish and impressive monastery. On more than one occasion he made reference to the former glories of the great monastery of Cluny, just a few miles away, over which the great St Odo presided in the tenth century. For generations it had been at the heart of monasticism and the centre of renewal and spiritual revival in mediaeval Europe. In the thirteenth century it was the largest church in Europe. Now it lies in ruins, a witness to past glory. Brother Roger was full of appreciation of the rich heritage of Cluny and spoke with great respect for its outstanding contribution to European Christianity. But he said that that was not Taizé's vocation. Whereas Cluny was a powerful religious community whose existence depended upon a large residential brotherhood, Taizé's aim is not to retain people but to send them back into the world. It is like a finger which points away from itself; it is content to give glory to God as if to say 'He is not here, he is risen. Seek him above; seek him in yourselves. Go from here and you will still find him.'

So one goes into the Church of Reconciliation. The atmosphere leaves no one neutral. It is always in semi-

darkness and yet the small spotlights and the candles —
hundreds of candles at the east end — forbid any thought of
gloom. The lights attract so that we are immediately drawn
away from ourselves to be with God and with others in
silence and stillness.

Perhaps one of the three formal services is about to begin.
There will be a feeling of almost tangible expectancy as the
stillness grows even deeper. And then you find that although
you are conscious of yourself in the great crowd, there is no
sense of feeling vulnerable, naked or alone. You don't
find yourself asking: 'What am I going to do now? What
religious acts am I expected to perform? Help! I don't know
what to do!' Somehow one catches the spirit of prayer. The
sheer fact that you sit on the floor and so adopt different
positions in the hope of finding comfort means there is little
uniformity in posture. There is no 'proper' thing to do.
That in itself is a liberating experience for Anglicans.
Perhaps we are the most self-conscious of all Christian
groups. We tend to go into church and cast furtive glances
at the person next to us. We sometimes worry about
secondary things like: 'Should we stand? Do I have to make
the sign of the cross like that man next to me?' At Taizé
people do their own thing but it is all right; there is no right
or wrong way of behaving. The simplicity seems to say:
'You are welcome; come as you are; be prepared for a few
surprises and let God take you as one dearly loved.'

We need to recover simplicity in our daily lives, our
behaviour and our church life. Taizé is a challenge to those
who measure things by a consumer culture. Those who join
the community commit themselves to simplicity of life.
They begin to learn the joy of sharing and giving to one
another. That is not God's way for all of us; but it is to
some. For those of us who are not called to stay in places

like Taizé the challenge is to live more simply. Eat less; consume less of the earth's precious resources; rely less on our computers, telephones, fax-machines and cars. Many of us are dominated by possessions. We find it hard to surrender life's goods. Let me be clear about this. There is nothing wrong in possessions as such. The point is – whom do they possess? If we use our possessions wisely and share them graciously they become tools. Obsessed by them, as some are, we become their slaves.

Taizé's attitude is conveyed by something that happened towards the end of the week. I wanted to give some money to the Community for its work. Brother Roger gently refused it, explaining that it is not Taizé's philosophy to receive money for itself. He believed it was essential for the Community to live from its work. Brothers never accept any donation or gift. Furthermore, in addition to the upkeep of the buildings, the Community of brothers shoulders the expenses incurred in welcoming young people from Eastern Europe, who have little means. In the early years, the Community accepted legacies which some brothers inherited. But then came a day when the family of one brother demanded that the inheritance be returned, claiming that it was part of the family heritage. The Community owed nothing to the family but Brother Roger believed, morally, that the sum demanded should be returned. The repayment lasted for some years and the event confirmed the decision never to accept anything, not even what brothers inherit. When I returned home I sent my gift to assist with their work in Bosnia.

The challenge is directed at church life as well as individual life-styles. It is easy to assume the world's standards of power, prestige and glory. Sometimes the Church is guilty of mistaking grandeur for grace. Sometimes we too are dominated by the 'clutter' of possessions. What Taizé teaches is the importance of those simple things we all know to be deeply important which are also the first to be overlooked. The importance of hospitality, the joy of laughter, the art of simple liturgy and songs that come from the heart. Taizé will never be remembered for its glamour and aesthetic beauty. It will always be treasured for the unadorned loveliness of human relationships found there, and the way we are loved in Christ.

Five

....

Journey in music

W orship is derived from the old word 'worth-ship'. This sums up accurately what we are doing when we worship God: we are expressing how much we value and love him, and what he means to us.

It is commonplace to find young people describing traditional church worship as 'boring'. This leads to a tendency to think that young people are simply not attracted to worship *per se*, or that the only forms of worship that will communicate are those clothed in the rock or pop culture of our times. Taizé however teaches us that young people are not alienated from worship itself. They find worship appealing provided it is worship-*ful* and includes them.

The elements of worship at Taizé are themselves traditional but it is the sense of expectation in worship which strikes some visitors as unusual. You sense that an encounter with God is possible, even likely. Some of those who accompanied me to Taizé contrasted this atmosphere with their churches at home — where little was expected and little preparation for worshipping God may have been done by priest or people.

Worship consists of many different elements. Praise, confession, contrition, prayer, hearing the Word of God in preaching and Scripture reading, feeding upon God sacramentally — and much more besides. Worship is a coat of many colours. It needs piecing together with care and imagination. Nothing is ever rushed at Taizé. That's a lesson in itself. And the seams of its worship are sown together by the music which integrates the whole.

Music in worship is universal. From time immemorial people have worshipped God by making music whether in basic rhythms or in a Mozart Mass. The Psalms are the song book of ancient Israel, and from them we glean that music accompanied the prayers and praise of the people of God: trumpet, sackbut and lyre along with other instruments were used to accompany worship. So the Psalmist says to God: 'I will sing a new song to you, O God: upon a ten stringed harp I will play to you' (Psalm 144.9).

What is music and why does it move us so? Music has been defined as 'a meaningful succession of perceptible sounds in temporal motion'. The philosopher Leibniz described music as 'a kind of counting performed by the mind without knowing that it is counting'. Such prosaic definitions hardly do justice to the sounds that can move our hearts and emotions more than words can express.

General Booth expressed it better: 'Music is to the song what wind is to the ship, blowing her onwards in the direction in which she is steered.' Music does have power to influence more deeply than we often realize.

At Taizé, the table talk that I and my party enjoyed every evening with Brother Roger and the brothers took us deeply into many aspects of worship and community life. On our second evening there the subject of singing came up naturally in our conversation. Brother Roger began: 'Music was part of our life from the very beginning. Music arises from a heart that loves. It comes from people in a special kind of relationship to God. It is a gift which comes from God but which we offer him.'

This intrigued me. How may a gift come from God and yet return to him again? The theme was picked up by one of the brothers who linked it with creation itself. Music is so universal a thing that it must originate from God himself. Its capacity to take us away from ourselves — expressing sadness, joy, gratitude and even ecstasy — conveys something of the mystery, beauty and order of God. 'People who love cannot help singing', stated one young brother, 'and those who love God have a song to sing.'

I pressed home the question: 'But how did the style of Taizé music develop? There must have been certain principles that guided your choice of material and the songs that emerged?'

Brother Roger refused to discuss music on its own. As the ministry of Taizé developed during the early days, he said, the brothers looked for a liturgy that was accessible to as many as possible. Because people usually came for just a short while, from many different traditions and language groups, it was essential to have worship that included everyone, with the emphasis upon simplicity.

Prayer at Taizé, continued Brother Roger, was and is inspired by the great monastic tradition: the chanting of psalms, Scripture readings, intercessions and prayers. There was no attempt or desire to pander to modern musical styles: Taizé's worship arises from the song of the Church. One brother told me: 'As people gather here from many diverse nations — France, Germany, Russia, England, Poland and many, many other places — we feel it is important that each person present can hear something in his or her own language, even if it is only a Bible verse.'

'Our problem during the early days', observed one of the older brothers, 'was how to allow everyone to participate in the singing of the Prayer when the great diversity of languages meant that very few could stay long enough to learn complex harmonies and master difficult words of unfamiliar languages.'

The result is unique. Taizé music and singing is unlike anything found in any other religious tradition. The brothers point out, though, that the roots of their music are in an age-old tradition of refrains, consisting of a few words of Scripture, set to music and sung as a canon or as an 'ostinato'. Throughout the centuries, a few words repeated over and over again have been a great assistance to contemplation, soothing the soul and lifting one to heights of joy and peace.

In this way the songs of Taizé were born. Brother Roger explained that the songs and chants originate in a number of different ways. They may arise from members of the Community who find that a song has arisen naturally in worship. But over the years a special relationship has developed between the brothers and a friend of the Community named Jacques Berthier whose compositional abilities are prized very highly by the brothers.

As I worshipped at the community I noticed several features of the singing that mark the style of Taizé. First, the *simplicity* of words and music which made it easy for us all to join in. The songs combine the traditions of East and West — plainchant may feature at one time, whilst at another the richer harmonies may evoke the breadth and richness of Orthodox worship. Indeed, the great value of the Taizé songs is not simply that the music fits the words so well, but that it takes into account the national flavour of the language originally used.

Simplicity applies to the word also. Short songs repeated over and over again allow basic gospel truths to penetrate the worshipper as an ongoing prayer. I noticed how time and again during the worship a chant might be sung for some minutes, the refrain and descant moving effortlessly along like a stream of prayer, a mantra of joy in the Lord. Because the simple musical themes and short phrases are easily learnt and have a tendency to remain with the singer long after audible sound has ceased, they meet the requirements to be both popular and contemplative. Indeed, they have no specified end and are brought to a conclusion only by the leader of the singing interposing an 'Amen!'

The words of the songs and chants are carefully chosen. What many appreciate is the objectivity of the statements addressed to God. This contrasts vividly with some modern songs which make statements about how we feel. They are sometimes difficult to sing with integrity. Not so Taizé songs. They pick up universal themes and often use the Great Words of the Church: Alleluia, Kyrie Eleison, Veni Creator Spiritus, and so on.

As we talked about Taizé worship with our groups the theme of worship back home came up time and again. 'Sometimes in my church at home', laughed one young man, 'I find myself thinking at times that you require a degree in music to appreciate what we are called upon to sing. But here at Taizé everyone can join in.' And so it is. The music is repetitive and no books are required and no great musical ability called for. The words are easily learned and thus much of the 'paper' end of liturgy is immediately taken out of worship and there is no rustling of paper or shutting of books when the song is ended.

But simplicity should never be confused with a slipshod and 'amateurish' approach to worship. Whilst all worship should aim to be simple, *thoroughness* must undergird its preparation. It is not surprising then that at Taizé the music is always rehearsed each afternoon by a volunteer choir who assist the brothers in charge of worship. As I worshipped alongside Brother Roger, towards the back of the ranks of white-robed brothers, I was very close to the young men who were given the special role of singing the descants which embellish the chants. I noticed the diligent and painstaking care in which the singing was conducted. None of the brothers concerned gave any suggestions that for them it was a performance. Their deportment and attitude showed very clearly that it was worship; they were absorbed by it yet sensitive to the needs of all worshippers. Indeed, a point often made, I understand, in rehearsal is that 'the music is always *for* the prayer'.

The songs and chants of Taizé, like any other Christian song or hymn, are never to be divorced from the whole act of worshipping God. They represent the offering of hearts to God in adoration, praise and submission. The words, taken from the Psalms, the Gospels or other parts of the Bible and the Christian tradition, are devoted to allowing God to speak to us and we to him. At first, in order to avoid too many of them being sung in French, Latin was used, and it quickly became a kind of 'lingua franca' at Taizé. Even for those who did not learn Latin at school, this is not even remotely a barrier. 'Ubi caritas et amor, Deus ibi est' ('Where charity and love are, God is there'). You don't have to be a classicist to recognize the words. But even if you are unfamiliar with them, this is no barrier at Taizé. The range of languages used in worship brings alive the international community gathered at Taizé. So, alongside familiar Latin chants like 'Jubilate Deo', 'Laudate Dominum' or 'Dona nobis pacem, Domine', you will hear songs in French like 'Mon âme se repose' or the Russian 'Gospodi' or the English 'O Lord hear my prayer'. One that made a great impression on many of us was a French song, 'Bénissez le Seigneur', which was sung with enthusiasm and meaning.

But we would be wrong to conclude from this that the centre of attention at Taizé is the emotional intensity of the music. It is not. The atmosphere of Taizé speaks of an attention given to the glory of God. It is noteworthy that hardened and seasoned young people, used to the up-beat rhythms of modern music with its concentration on emotion, very quickly realize that at Taizé music performs a quite different service. It is a servant, a handmaid, for the worship of Almighty God. It has no value on its own.

Of course this does not mean that everything is perfect with respect to Taizé singing and chanting or that everyone appreciates it. One young man from England found some difficulties with it after a few days. 'It's so monotonous', he complained. 'The songs sometimes go on for hours!' He received a straightforward reply from a girl in his discussion group: 'No, "monotonous" is the wrong word to use', she retorted. 'It is *repetitive* and you have to learn *how* to use repetition. If you struggle to keep singing all the time you may not be paying attention to what God is saying to you *through* the time of worship. You don't have to sing all the time to be part of it. You don't have to make a huge effort! Relax; imagine it to be an escalator which draws you close to God.'

I thought at the time that the girl's image of singing as a kind of escalator was a very helpful and accurate idea. Our mistake, often, is to think of worship as *my* work instead of the work of the *whole Church*. All we are doing when we worship is to enter into the Church's offering of praise and worship. One of the lessons of Taizé is that it helps us to see ourselves as part of an act of worship. There will be times when the worship leads us deeper into private prayer and as our lips fall silent others around us keep the prayer and praise going. This discovery can lead to a deeper appreciation of more traditional forms of worship. To find that you can be led more profoundly into prayer whilst others continue to sing, and that *their* singing is the means, is simply to discover a truth the Church has always known. Sometimes people express impatience that they cannot 'join in' the worship of a cathedral where the choir sings everything. Yet there are other levels of participation. Listening to the beauty of the singing of a well-trained choir giving expression to music which few amateur choirs can attain is a form of worship when we enter into it with our hearts. Taizé enables many to understand this and encourages them to join in at whatever level they feel comfortable with.

However, Taizé music manages to be both popular and contemplative. Its simplicity means that it is accessible. Yet it is never loud or intrusive. The blasting of the eardrum — the perennial complaint of all parents about young people's music — has no place at Taizé. Those from charismatic Evangelical traditions sometimes find Taizé forbiddingly restrained at first. It isn't what they are used to or expect. The majority, however, very quickly come to enjoy it and take it home to contribute to the life of their communities because of its obvious Christ-centred accent.

As I have already observed, another common complaint that gets 'turned on its head' at Taizé concerns repetition in Christian worship. 'It's always the same', said a girl about her church services at home. Yet at Taizé the same words are often said or sung again and again — and yet again! The prayer of repetition is more deeply rooted in the universal religious psyche than we realize. Jesus gave us just a single prayer to be said over and over again. We have not grown tired of the Lord's Prayer over the centuries because we know its truths are timeless and its richness is beyond description. Brother Roger shared with me his discovery of the power of simple prayers repeated over and over again. For some it might be the Jesus Prayer — 'Lord, have mercy on me a sinner'. For others it might be 'Hail Mary, full of grace'. A simple meditative prayer I use on occasions is one that focuses on the names of Christ: 'Jesus, Word of God — fill your Church with your living Word; Jesus, Bread of Life, feed me with your presence; Jesus, true Vine, help me to abide in you; Jesus, the way, the truth and the life — help me to live your life today' . . . and so on.

One of the most special times at Taizé is *after* the evening service. As the service ends some of the brothers leave for various domestic duties while Brother Roger and some of the brothers responsible for the singing move to the front of the church. The singing may continue for another long period of time but no one is in a hurry to leave — the place seems to fall into a deeper level of praise and rejoicing. In the light of the many candles the young people around me are lost in God, sprawled on the ground in many different positions, lost, as the hymn puts it 'in wonder, love and praise'. And then Brother Roger and some of the Community will withdraw and go to the back of the church to be available for the young people. An information leaflet given to all visitors explains that they are there '. . . to listen to you. If you want to speak about something that hurts you or which obstructs the paths of a search for the living God, some brothers remain in the Church after the evening prayer.' The brothers say how amazed they are by the many people who do want to talk and the many more who stay behind in the church simply for prayer, meditation and worship. No one is in a hurry at Taizé — unless it is in a hurry to do business with God.

MUSIC IN WORSHIP

Music is crucially important for worship and there is much that Taizé has to teach the wider Church. As I have observed, many young people find the worship of their parish churches more a barrier to spiritual growth than a help. Very few parish priests and leading lay people recognize that the criticisms of young people may be very well founded. We do well to pay attention to what they are saying to us. The impact of Taizé music on young people should be carefully considered by us all and the lessons learned. As I reflected upon this I saw the following areas of great importance for the European Churches.

1. The acceptance of different styles. Although Taizé has its own distinctive style, it readily recognizes the validity of many different forms of musical expression. The brothers uttered many warnings to people who wanted to take Taizé music back home. 'Be very careful', I heard one young brother urge a group. 'What may work and fire you here may not have quite that impact back in your youth club. Don't forget that music at Taizé has its context in *our* worshipping life and the atmosphere of thousands of young people gathered together with gifted instrumentalists and singers. Be very careful how you apply Taizé music — or you may be very disappointed.'

That is a warning we must heed. But Taizé music is of

course translatable because its simplicity makes it accessible for even the most modest of choirs or music groups. Indeed, it is so much part of world-wide Christianity now that we are likely to encounter Taizé songs in a sleepy country church or a charismatic prayer fellowship. I heard the story of an Irish boy visiting Taizé for the first time to discover to his pleasure that the Community were singing the songs of — his church!

Taizé music, well done and well prepared, can enrich worship wherever we are. When I was enthroned as Archbishop of Canterbury the prayers were punctuated by a group of singers singing a Taizé song. Many viewers wrote in to say how much they appreciated that part of the service. The average parish choir could quickly be taught to sing the songs and chants of Taizé, including some of the more intricate descants. English Christians in particular have been eclectic in their music. Our hymns reflect this — Graham Kendrick may sit alongside John Henry Newman, Charles Wesley and St Ambrose of Milan.

That is why it is natural to affirm the importance of variety of styles of music in church life. A sign of a growing and adapting church is in its ability to keep literally in tune culturally with its society. Anglicans have much to learn from the charismatic and house churches just as we do from traditional forms of worship. The music of Graham Kendrick is now very well known, as I have mentioned, and young people sing his songs with great feeling and joy: we should not despise and reject what others find spiritually helpful.

Occasionally I've met a regrettable tendency to despise the use of various modern music instruments in worship as if there is something doctrinally correct about the use of piano and organ in worship but considerable doubt about other instruments. I am encouraged by the increasing number of music groups alongside organs and traditional choirs. Let's be more inclusive.

I repeat: this does not rule out traditional forms. Not all that is modern is good; and not all that is old is bad. I love the choral tradition which the English Church has made famous and so distinctively its own. I sincerely hope we do not lose this rich tradition of glorious choral singing. I love too the stirring poetry of the hymns of Isaac Watts, Charles Wesley, John Newton and John Henry Newman and the music which in so many respects has helped to make them so memorable. I can even appreciate a great number of Sankey's Revival hymns. And as we recall the history of sacred music we need to remember that virtually all the hymns we now call traditional, and part of every church's repertoire, were once brand new and many had their critics even then!

2. Music as a servant of the Church's mission. We have already noticed the powerful, evocative influence of music, whether it is the haunting qualities of a popular song or the glorious and heavenward-soaring delights of Mozart's Piano Concerto in C. People will go miles and pay generously for good music: such is its spell over us.

The Church has known this for a long time. In its history music has had a long and distinguished place. Mention has already been made of Mozart. He, together with other great musicians like Handel and Bach, composed music for the Church and its worship. I recall a visit to Cape Town when I preached at the Holy Communion service in the cathedral at which the music was Mozart's Coronation Mass. The cathedral choir and orchestra, consisting almost entirely of good amateurs, offered their praise to God through this rendering of Mozart's great work. It was a wonderful and unforgettable act of worship. Afterwards the Dean told me that every month the choir make a similar offering in worship as part of their contribution to the Decade of Evangelism. People come from miles around because of the splendid combination of Christian worship and glorious music. I thought at the time what a truly 'evangelical' occasion it was, bringing many people into church for an inspiring service. Music — whether traditional or contemporary — can be the means of bringing people into contact with the things of God. We should be grateful that music touches people in deep and mysterious ways, for it has power to lead them to faith in Christ.

The same, of course, is true of other musical styles. We are well aware of the drawing power of rock musicians and pop-artists who appeal to the young. The Church cannot afford to be distant from these forms or contemptuous of those who have gifts to influence youth culture. We must learn to communicate to our rising generation the wonder of worshipping God. The 'Nine O'Clock' service at St Thomas', Crookes, in Sheffield is a good example of Christian vision combined with imaginative appropriation of youth culture and music. We may think also of Christian festivals like Greenbelt and pilgrimage centres like Iona where the range of contemporary music is shown to be much wider than many people think.

To return to Taizé's special contribution, we have an excellent illustration of how God can take what is simple and good and use it to his glory. For one of our English pilgrims the songs of Taizé became the bridge of faith. She explained that one day in her church the choir sang a Taizé song and suddenly, she said, the place was filled with a new song: 'I felt caught up in what seemed a strange song. It was

"Magnificat". Just one word sung over and over. Men and women's voices mixing and separating with a lovely descant floating over the top. It spoke to me in a way that no other church music has done.' It resulted in her drawing closer to God and eventually she made her pilgrimage with me to Taizé to sing the songs in the place where it all began!

That story will not startle those of us who have experienced the sound of Taizé. It might even encourage those of us who are responsible for worship to realize that to many people music can be the way God speaks to them. It has power to lead people very close to the living God.

3. Music is a servant of 'word' and worship.   Music can be a powerful stimulant as well as having great powers to soothe. The troubled Saul in the Old Testament found David's playing of the lyre exquisitely beautiful. We have all known moments of great wonder when we have listened to great music.

But like all of God's gifts music can be trivialized and abused when its function is distorted. I am annoyed when I go into department stores where music is employed as a kind of 'wallpaper'. Its function seems to be limited to providing a pleasant, harmless background noise. It is often not loud enough to hear and not quiet enough to be ignored. Sometimes music is employed deliberately because of its hypnotic powers. Even in church life its powers to anaesthetize may be devised to stimulate emotions and stop people thinking.

It is vital then that those who conduct worship should consider carefully *why* and on *what* basis they are choosing music. Words and music must match. Planning for worship must commence with the nature of the service and then go on to consider what form of music suits the occasion best.

Perhaps now we are beginning to appreciate General Booth's retort to a man who accused the young Salvation Army of 'pinching' secular tunes: 'I rather enjoy robbing the Devil of his choice tunes', commented General Booth. 'Music is about the best commodity he possesses.' While this may be so, we should avoid the temptation to start from the music and then form worship around it. Music is a tool, a servant, and words and tunes must be chosen with care in the light of the theme and thrust of the worship we want to offer God.

This however raises the question of standards: is there such a thing as 'bad' music or is it a case of beauty in the eye of the beholder, or the 'ear' of the listener? I am sure there will be many who believe that there is a definite standard of excellence that makes it possible for us to access quality in music. In church life our choices are often limited by such factors as the limitations of musicians available to us, the aesthetic qualities of the buildings and, perhaps most significant of all, the nature of the congregation and the purpose of the music we are about to choose.

It therefore seems to me that we who are engaged in offering worship to God must aim for that excellence that gives him glory. Of course, it probably will fall a long way short of the professional musician — but that will not matter. What matters is the spirit we put into it, the thoroughness and the enthusiasm which will make this offering pass from performance into worship. But the congregation and its needs should be kept in mind. The diversity of preferences places a great burden on those responsible for worship. I do not agree with those who say that styles of music will not mix. From rich experience in parish ministry where I worked with both choir and music group I can say without hesitation that a mixture of styles often works superbly well. What matters is having musicians and singers who are prepared to be adaptable and in this most subjective of all disciplines to have humility and kindness one to another.

Variety, then, in musical expression may often be required of us in church life but not at the expense of quality. I recall the painfulness of enduring a service of worship in a country church where a person was asked by the incumbent to play the organ at short notice. As he was forced protestingly to play, the resulting performance must have been a sore embarrassment to him and an offence to our eardrums. A said service would have been far better. Poor rendering of hymns and music can distract a congregation and diminish worship. Yet, we all know and acknowledge the opposite — the pleasure of hearing good music sung really well, the effortless singing of a well-trained choir and the majestic chords of an organist and musicians who are offering to the glory of God, and to the church, the fruits of their practice.

Taizé is associated with music — simple music sung from the heart, music well done and well presented. But attention is never drawn to the music at Taizé. It is there as an offering to God and as an aid to worship. No one fêtes the singers and no one seeks to perform. Worship is offered for the purpose, as one of the songs states: 'Adoramus te, Christe'. The intention, in the words of F. W. Faber, is that the 'music of the Gospel may lead us home'.

Six

....

Journey into the Eucharist

As we have already seen, Taizé is a place where people find God in many different ways. It is not unusual at Taizé to find people constantly reflecting on spiritual experience and discussing how God discloses himself to us. One evening I focused on that precise question and asked one diocesan group: 'How does God reveal himself to people at this place? Has he spoken to you in any particular way?'

The responses were predictably varied: through worship, through silent prayer, through the Bible and discussion groups, through friendship across cultural and language barriers. Many spoke with appreciation of new insights discovered and new experiences of God gained. However, we entered new territory when a girl observed thoughtfully: 'I believe that at the heart of Taizé is the presence of God in the Eucharist. For me that has been one of the most precious times of all. My appreciation of Holy Communion has deepened through the daily celebration.'

At first a number of her friends questioned her claim. The Eucharist did not seem to them to dominate Taizé's life and worship. Their friend's statement seemed rather extraordinary and contrary to the experience of most of the English pilgrims.

I raised this matter with Brother Roger one afternoon: 'Is the Eucharist central to Taizé and its life? Is it, actually, the heart of the community life as that girl believed?'

Brother Roger replied, saying that indeed the Eucharist is at the heart of the vocation to reconciliation and he told me a story which remains very vivid in his memory. In 1970 he made a visit to Patriarch Athenagoras in Constantinople. They had already met several times, and this was to prove their very last encounter (the Patriarch died in 1972). When the time of departure came, as Brother Roger was leaving him, the Patriarch, standing in the doorway, raised his hands in the gesture of elevating the chalice and said these final words: 'The cup and the breaking of bread. There is no other solution. Remember that.'

The Eucharist is central in Taizé. However, the Community respects the tradition of those who come to Taizé and makes sure that each person can receive communion according to their own custom. This care for the diversity of the pilgrims is expressed in a notice board at the entrance of the Church of Reconciliation. One of the brothers drew my attention to it. Written in six languages, it says:

> Catholic Mass is celebrated each day in different places. The Blessed Sacrament is reserved next to the icon of the Virgin Mary. It is from there that the Catholic Communion is distributed every morning.
>
> For those from the Churches of the Reformation, the Lord's Supper is celebrated every day. Every morning, they can receive the Lord's Supper at the entrance to the Anglican Chapel, to the right of the icon of the Resurrection.

Orthodox Mass is celebrated periodically.
For those who do not receive communion, there is blessed
bread, which everyone can receive.

Brother Roger underlines this last provision. For those
who, for a variety of reasons, do not feel it right to receive
Holy Communion, 'blessed bread' is available. This innova-
tion, based on Orthodox practice (and interestingly also an
ancient custom in certain Catholic parishes locally in
Burgundy) is another example of Taizé's spirit of generosity
and hospitality. They do not want anyone to feel excluded.
So even those who feel themselves to be 'outside' the faith
can take the blessed bread which carries no obligation to
conform in belief.

In Taizé the communion is nevertheless a 'converting
ordinance'. Offering each pilgrim the possibility of receiving
communion every day is a call to walk the way of the cross
in newness of life. It is a stunning revelation to so many –
and young people no less – spending hours and hours in
church. Although there are many sitting or kneeling in
quiet corners of the huge building, you will see some
kneeling before the Orthodox icon or before the 'Real
Presence'. Some may think this borders on superstition.
'Surely', they might say, 'God cannot be confined to icons,
tabernacles or religious buildings.' I agree. God is with us
everywhere we go. He is with us when we pray at home;
when we read Scripture, when we worship in our churches
or serve him in his world. The Incarnation of our Lord
demonstrates clearly that in a fundamental sense everything
is sacred and nothing is secular. We cannot confine God to
religious buildings or religious acts. It was Archbishop
William Temple who described Christianity as 'the most
materialistic of all religions'.

But this truth certainly does not repudiate the importance of holy places which help us to focus on God's activity in the world. There are places which God has hallowed through the celebration of the Eucharist day by day and week by week. It is also certain, as we saw earlier, that devotional objects like icons assist our prayer life by enabling us to focus on the God we adore who defies all our attempts to contain him.

What makes holy places 'holy' would constitute a study in itself. But there are places which have an aura, an atmosphere, a presence which we associate with holiness. It is always something which we can only describe as OTHER. God is as close to us as our very being, yet also separate, set apart. This paradox is evident at Taizé. God is known in community and communion, yet he must not be confused with any particular community. He is Wholly Other; the One to be worshipped and adored.

This otherness of God is expressed not least in the way in which everyone in the Church of Reconciliation faces east to worship. Community and congregation alike look towards the altar and beyond where flickering candles represent the mystery and otherness of God. It is fascinating to recall that here at Taizé, this community, which began its life with brothers from Protestant backgrounds, has resisted the iconoclastic tendencies associated with some aspects of the Reformation. Rather, it encourages all ways of worship and all legitimate aids that will lead young people closer to God.

Holy places are places of remembrance. They recall how God has chosen — in word, sacrament, healing or revelation — to meet his people there in a special way. 'Do this in remembrance of me' said Jesus. He calls his followers to be a remembering people. In this sense 'home' and 'church' may overlap. Just as our homes are associated with our memories, our achievements, our deepest relationships and our greatest longings, so the holy place similarly is invested with the memories of grace-filled moments and the life-giving relationship which continues to shape us. Holy places are not to be treated as of no account. They will always matter to those who have met God or who have yielded to his will in a certain place. Indeed, it is right to call such places of revelation 'sacramental' because grace has been given and received there.

But the holy place is not a cultic secret to be kept to ourselves, even though some congregations seem to want to keep the 'good news' to themselves. Places for remembering are also places for telling, for proclaiming what God has done, for sharing with others what we have seen and known and discovered.

Taizé is a place of remembering and of telling. In vivid contrast to many religious communities it makes no secret of its desire for pilgrims to return home with the message of God's love. Its whole *raison d'être* is streamlined to make this effective. Central to this vision is that young people will return to their home churches charged with new appreciation of what the faith means and with a deeper commitment to it. Initially, many young people feel irritation with their home churches when they compare them to Taizé. Gradually, though, a different spirit often prevails and an appreciation grows of *all* places that God has made holy with his presence.

I spent much time reflecting on all this in the weeks that followed our pilgrimage. Two aspects of his 'presence' merit attention. First, that of his presence with us whenever Christians gather. At Taizé there was an expectancy

about the worship which was clearly based on this understanding. At this level we must be discouraged from
narrowing the focus. Christ is present where his word
is preached and read; where people sing his praises and sink
into profound silence before him. I spoke to a friend about
how pilgrims are offered the possibility of receiving
communion every day in Taizé. This makes people aware
of the 'ordinariness' of daily communion. There seemed
something so matter-of-fact about it. After a little silence he
said, 'Yes, I agree, there is an "ordinariness" about the daily
communion at Taizé, but it is a "filled" ordinariness. It
arises from something extraordinary. It reflects the community itself — a community in which God is present.
From that experience of living with God, worship emerges
with a great power. So very ordinary but so very
extraordinary at the same time.'

My friend's response reminded me of Dietrich Bon-
hoeffer's great statement about how people encounter
Christ in the church:

> Jesus is present as the crucified and risen one . . . *Present* is to
> be understood in a temporal and spatial sense, 'hic et nunc'.
> Christ is present in the Church as a person. Only because
> Christ is present can we enquire of him . . . only because
> preaching and sacrament take place in church can Christ be
> sought after. The understanding of his presence opens the
> way for the understanding of the person.

I believe that the discovery of true community is a
discovery of Christ. Here lies one of the greatest challenges
facing Western Christianity today. Our patterns of devotion
have been so individualistic that we have missed this basic
truth. What so many young people discover at Taizé is the
experience of genuine Christian community. And through

that community the living Christ is met. It is hardly surprising that worship and fellowship there takes on such an intensity for young people. It is equally natural that young people, like Peter on the Mount of Transfiguration, either want to stay there forever or, alternatively, want to take the Taizé experience home 'lock, stock and barrel'. It is not simply the singing and the chanting that people miss when they return home — they miss 'the Church'. Their experience of Christian fellowship and therefore of the presence of Christ has been so overwhelming that they cannot abide the sterility of what they had before and to which they must return. This issue is like an unexploded bomb for all European Churches today. A great gulf separates the traditional understanding of ecclesiology and that of the younger generation whose experience of human associations are much more individualistic, transitory and less rooted. Taizé does try to prepare people for their return home. Many make the transference well. But often in the home churches people scarcely wish to hear of their experience, little realizing that a 'new song' is being sung among them.

But let us consider a second aspect of 'presence': that of the presence of Christ encountered in the elements of bread and wine in the Eucharist. Perhaps here more than in most areas of theology we are up against the limits of language in expressing deep truth. On the one hand there is nothing very special about 'bread' and 'wine'. Their significance lies, of course, when we use them in a particular way and for a special reason. We fully comprehend this in many social contexts. Take a wedding anniversary. A couple may want to commemorate their relationship by having a meal together with a good bottle of wine. Without being conscious of it, their celebration takes on an almost sacramental flavour as they go back over the memories, linger over good and bad times and toast the future.

Similar elements are present when Christians gather to celebrate the Eucharist. However, there are significant differences. Three features in particular must be isolated if we are to understand fully what is going on.

First, it is the Church's celebration. The congregation, as the People of God, gathers to remember and to share in Christ's victory over sin and death. Properly speaking, the Risen Christ is the host at this meal but the recipients of it are the whole people of God. Second, while it remains the priestly activity of the Church to celebrate the victory of the cross, certain people are 'ordained' to preside over the communal meal. We call them 'priests' because they act for us and for the Risen Christ in setting forth the fruits of his grace. They represent the whole people of God as, together, we celebrate the finished sacrifice of our High Priest. Third, following the example of our Lord the rightful elements of bread and wine are taken and used. The time-hallowed words of Institution are used over the bread and wine: 'Take and eat this . . . drink this . . . in remembrance of Me.'

These three features — the People of God, the ministers who are apart to celebrate on behalf of the congregation, and the elements of bread and wine — become the living dynamic in which Christ makes himself known to us. It is a mistake to make any particular element dominate.

In recent years, dialogue between the Churches, particularly between Roman Catholics and Anglicans, has made it clear that, underlying our differing doctrinal approaches which we have inherited from the past, there exists a common faith in Christ's real presence in the Eucharist. Bread and wine retain the properties of bread and wine.

But they do not remain merely bread and wine. Sacramentally, they become for us the body and blood of our Lord. They are charged with a greater significance. They are received with thankful hearts because they convey to our waiting souls the life transforming effects of the victory of the cross. The celebrant asks God in the Thanksgiving Prayer that 'the bread and wine may become *for us the body and blood of our Lord Jesus Christ*'. The language of 'becoming' does not imply any material change. Rather (to quote the words of the Anglican–Roman Catholic International Commission) 'what is here affirmed is a sacramental presence in which God uses realities of this world to convey the realities of the new creation: bread for this life becomes the bread of eternal life. Before the eucharistic prayer, to the question: "What is that?", the believer answers: "It is bread." After the eucharistic prayer, to the same question he answers: "It is truly the body of Christ, the Bread of Life."' That is why, according to Anglican tradition, if any of the consecrated bread and wine is left over after the communion, the priest is required to consume the remainder reverently — it must not be disposed of as if it were simply bread and wine.

But let us consider here two key words in Eucharistic doctrine: 'remembering' and 'faith'. What is the Church doing when it remembers what Christ had done? What is the content of belief?

We are handicapped by our understanding of 'remembering'. It means for most people 'recalling a past event'. To return to the illustration of a couple celebrating their wedding anniversary: they may well recall the great day and all the different elements which made it so memorable. This is in great contrast with the biblical idea of remembering as expressed in the Greek word *anamnesis* which conveys the idea of being present 'as if we were there personally'. The background is the Jewish Passover. At that central act of Jewish faith the youngest child present asks a series of questions of the host:

> Why is this night different from any other night?
> On any other night we eat leavened and unleavened bread. Why on this night only unleavened bread?
> On any other night we eat any kind of herbs. Why tonight only bitter herbs?
> On any other night we do not dip our herbs into anything even once. Why on this night do we dip it twice?
> On any other night we eat sitting upright or reclining. Why on this night do we all recline?

The answer given by the father of the household is startling in its personalizing of Jewish history.

> Because slaves *we were* to Pharaoh in Egypt and the Lord our God *brought us out of there* with a mighty hand . . .

It is central to the story of their redemption for the Jews of every generation to enter into the Passover ritual as though they were among the Hebrews in the land of Egypt. For Christians, too, the events of Calvary are not simply 'back there'. At every Eucharist we are not worshippers who try to remember what Christ has done and who treat the story as if it happened long ago for the sins of all. We enter into the story as participants. The Eucharist tells the Christian story that Christ's victory is our victory. His sacrifice is set forth afresh and becomes contemporaneous with us.

But we do not overlook the importance of faith in

receiving. This is true of most traditions. Our personal response is crucial. If we do not bring to the Eucharist our willingness to receive the gift of life, we shall walk away empty. The Eucharist means nothing to unbelieving hearts. It cannot convey grace to those who are indifferent, careless or apathetic. We receive him by faith but no less really than if he were with us in the room. We leave strengthened by grace given; partakers of his 'once for all' salvation offered on the cross — its benefits released as we in obedience do this 'in remembrance of Me'.

'Remembering' and 'faith' are brought together in a dynamic way in the works of Richard Hooker, one of our greatest Anglican theologians. Hooker lived at the time of the English Reformation and was closely involved in the reconstruction of the English Church. He had no wish to deny the reality of the presence of Christ in the Eucharist but there was necessity at that time to assert the importance of believing faith. Hooker states: 'The real presence of Christ's most blessed body and blood is not to be sought for in the sacrament, but in the worthy receiver of the sacrament.' This doctrine, known as 'receptionism', does not in fact deny that Christ is really present in the sacrament but is intended to emphasize the point that the sacraments are meant to be used – they convey God's grace *really* to our hearts. However, classical Anglicanism tends to go beyond receptionism in recognizing the *objectivity* of the sacrament. The subjectivity of 'my' faith meets the objectivity of Christ's gift to me in the sacrament of Holy Communion. Real grace is imparted and the presence of Christ known and experienced to the embrace of faith. As Anglican and Roman Catholic theologians have agreed: 'The bread and wine *become* the sacramental body and blood of Christ in order that the Christian community may become more truly what it already is, the body of Christ.' Wisest of all, perhaps, was Queen Elizabeth I of England, who summed up the meaning of communion in a little verse with which Christians of all traditions can identify:

> 'Twas God the word that spake it,
> He took the Bread and brake it;
> And what the word did make it;
> That I believe, and take it.

The important link I detected at Taizé between the Eucharist and Communion reminded me very much of an insight which John Wesley developed over 200 years ago. In 1733 he preached a remarkable sermon pleading for 'constant communion'. It was a counter to the prevailing trend in the eighteenth century which argued that you had to prepare long and hard to receive Holy Communion. This tendency assumed a high state of piety but, in Wesley's opinion, might discourage those who were lowly and humble of heart. At that time Wesley would not have dreamed it possible or even desirable that the majority of Christians communicate daily, though he himself often did so more than once a week. But what he did understand was that the only absolutely necessary preparation for Holy Communion was to come willingly to receive what Christ offered to all people. He knew that those who received Christ's body were built into the body of Christ, and that receiving communion strengthened the bonds of Christian community.

More than that, Wesley believed that it was in receiving Holy Communion that the Christian experienced the benefits of salvation at a level beyond description. It changed people. Or, in Wesley's words, it was a 'converting ordinance'. Wesley wrote:

The prayer, the fast, the word conveys,
When mixed with faith, Thy life to me;
In all the channels of thy grace
I still have fellowship with Thee:
But chiefly here my soul is fed
With fullness of immortal bread.

It was customary in Wesley's time to regard the Holy Communion as a 'confirming ordinance'. That is to say, as a means by which a Christian grew in faith after conversion and baptism. At that period it was not only Catholics and Anglicans who restricted access to the sacrament. Baptists, Congregationalists and Presbyterians generally admitted only the converted to communion. While John Wesley was deeply sympathetic to that theology, he pressed on beyond it. He saw the Holy Communion as a means of grace that actually led to conversion in those that had hearts open to the call of Christ.

So the Eucharist is very special to all Christians and central to the life of the Taizé community. Like the Eucharist itself, which brings together the natural and the spiritual, so Taizé is a very down-to-earth place. It possesses a *holy worldliness* which so many young people find refreshing. I mentioned earlier that in one sense the community's Eucharist seemed very 'ordinary'. But isn't this description exactly what we should expect? We live at a time in the West where a chasm lies between religious experience and everyday life. 'Going to church' seems to so many people a journey into irrelevance, an experience that takes them 'out of the world' and away from real events. At

Taizé a bridge is built between the two worlds and they are united in a natural understanding that both belong to God and matter to him. Of course, at one level Taizé is *deeply religious*. You cannot escape the fact that life revolves around worship. The atmosphere is charged with a spirituality that is undeniable and unmistakable. But at another level it isn't religious at all. People act as if going to church and worshipping, singing and acts of piety are the most ordinary and natural things to do. There is no embarrassment about religion at Taizé. Even wholly secular people who suddenly find themselves in the Community take the life of the place in their stride.

This again is a parable of the Eucharist. When we celebrate the Eucharist we are recalling the most amazing event in the life of our planet: God took human form for us and died for us. He died to bring us to God and lives within us to bring peace, joy and hope to others. Thus at this most fundamental level, the Eucharist is very 'worldly' indeed. It is given for the world; it is celebrated in the world using the elements of bread and wine — simple earthy things — which are taken and filled with God's presence.

The 'ordinariness' of Taizé's Eucharist is therefore a telling parable of the way we should live day by day. The bread broken and wine shared take us naturally from the shared living of Christian community to the places where God appears to be absent, those places of suffering which seem to mock his very existence. But Calvary reminds us he is there already. We go to join him in the world's suffering to be his body. By going there as his body, we make him known by witness to others and by his grace sanctify the normal, the ordinary, and the trivial. The ordinariness of the sacrament tells us that nothing that God creates is worthless or beyond redemption. The Church is that body which lives out its existence in a holy worldliness for its Lord. Again, Taizé has sought to explore this in its living. The brothers do not live in isolated, protected space at Taizé. Not only are they invaded gladly by hordes of pilgrims each year but the brothers are to be found throughout the world in the poorest and most dangerous of places. The eyes of Taizé are open to the calamities of life. My talks with Brother Roger revealed a man who was steeped in prayer but who knew what was going on in the world around. Prayer was never divorced from the pain and agony of others.

Yet another seemingly ignored aspect of the Eucharist that Taizé often communicates to people is that of joy awakened in their hearts. One afternoon at tea time I walked through the crowded main thoroughfare of Taizé and encountered a group of people from Poland and Russia. Even though we had no common language we managed to communicate through a few English words and through the universal language of smiles, gesticulations and the occasional passing interpreter. Each person from these two countries had stories to share of hardship and persecution. One man in his thirties had been imprisoned for his faith; another, a teacher by profession, had found that promotion had been denied because his views as a Christian were 'incompatible' with the secular views of the State. I asked them for their opinion of life now in their countries. The reaction was predictably volatile. They were all agreed that economically the problems were immense but, said one lady with sparkling eyes, the essential difference is that they now possess freedom. 'We are free once more, free to think and to be free. Free to worship and share our Christian faith with others. Our countries are experiencing an awakening of joy!' They could not adequately state in words, they said, what Taizé had meant to them. They were over-whelmed by the wonder of the Christian faith and encouraged by the fellowship and love.

The phrase 'awakening of joy' stuck with me as I left them. Taizé has had that experience for so many and I believe that it still calls the Church to a 'reawakening of celebration' today — not only in Eastern Europe as it struggles to throw off the shackles of Communism but the apathy and materialism of Western Europe.

But why do we find that in so many countries the Eucharist is not a celebration, a thanksgiving and an explosion of joy at all but often the very opposite? I recall attending a Cathedral Eucharist a few years ago and the service was so joyless and gloomy that a stranger could have easily assumed it was a funeral service. Of course, there has to be proper reverence. That is agreed, but reverence does not mean such solemnity that smiles, joyful singing and vigorous participation are absent.

This vision is being lived at Taizé. The Polish and Russian pilgrims I met that afternoon were in no doubt about the joy they were experiencing in the worship and with one another. The community, as a community of prayer, drew all who worshipped there to a deeper unity. At one level denominational differences were reduced to a profound unity in Christ. Although I was recognizable as the Archbishop of Canterbury, I was welcomed as a brother Christian. Anglican pilgrims were welcomed not because they were Anglicans but because they were fellow pilgrims in need of God and his love. Distinctive theological labels which separate Christians like 'Catholic', 'evangelical', 'liberal' and 'charismatic' were not so much avoided as unnecessary. Taizé made us all equal with and for one another. Little wonder then that celebration is such a key note at Taizé and little wonder that many return from Taizé reawakened in joy and faith.

But the Eucharist is and remains 'Thanksgiving' because it represents the fullness of Christian joy at the heart of creation and salvation. Here we have to understand that theologically it spans the past, present and future. Past, because we can look back with deep thankfulness to what God has done for us in creation and salvation. That past event irradiates our present with the presence of the Lord; he is with us whenever we take bread and wine. Then the past and present give meaning and hope to the future. Living as we do in a world where meaning and hope are conspicuously absent, the Christian faith has tremendous power to give life and purpose. Taizé is not alone in witnessing to this strength. But what it particularly points to is a spirituality which, focused on the Eucharist, is the true heart of prayer. Bishop Mervyn Stockwood put it so well when he wrote 'I think of the Mass as a golden cord that begins at Bethlehem, proceeds to Calvary and the Easter Garden, continues through the joys and sufferings of mankind till it reaches the Kingdom of God'.

Seven

······························

Journey into discovering God's will

Towards the end of our week at Taizé a dramatic event occurred in the evening worship which I am sure had a great impact on many. During the service a young African was received into the Community as a 'young brother'. It was a simple and moving ceremony. In the packed but totally hushed Church of Reconciliation, Brother Roger clothed him with the community's white robe, saying 'My dear brother, without looking back, you want to follow Christ, so remember that Christ murmurs in the silence of your heart "Do not be afraid, I am there". The Risen Christ loves you like his only one, he will love you for ever, that is his secret.'

At the end of the prayer, Brother Roger explained to everyone present what was happening. 'What does it mean to receive this white robe? It means that our young brother is going to prepare himself to offer his entire existence to Christ. He will live as a celibate. He will be available day after day to create a parable of community with his brothers. He will also seek to accomplish the work of Christ, "Go and sell what you have and give it to the poor, then come and follow me!" For us, the fact of not receiving gifts or individual bequests or anything at all sets us on the way of great simplicity. We are well aware that no one is built by nature to accomplish such a "yes". For those who follow Christ, there are moments of inner struggle. And so the way forward is this: surrendering ourselves in humble trust that Christ lives within us through his Holy Spirit.'

The next day Brother Roger and I talked again. He told me that in Taizé the period of preparation for a new brother lasts several years but there is no formal novitiate because individuals mature at different rates. It is a matter for the individual brother and for the community to decide when he is ready to be 'professed' — that is, to take his life-long vows.

I was not present at a life 'profession' but I was told that the ceremony was longer and even more impressive than the entry into the community. At the profession itself, there is a dialogue between Brother Roger and the brother who is making his commitment:

'Will you, for love of Christ, consecrate yourself to him with all your being?'
'I will.'
'Will you henceforth fulfil your service of God within our community, in communion with your brothers?'
'I will.'
'Will you, renouncing all ownership, live with your brothers not only in community of material goods, but also in community of spiritual goods, striving for openness of heart?'
'I will.'
'Will you, in order to be more available to serve with your brothers, and in order to give yourself in undivided love to Christ, remain in celibacy?'

'I will.'
'Will you, so that we may be of one heart and one mind and so that the unity of our common service may be fully achieved, adopt the orientations of the community expressed by the prior, bearing in mind that he is only a poor servant in the community?'
'I will.'
'Will you, always discerning Christ in your brothers, watch over them in good days and bad, in suffering and in joy?'
'I will.'

As I studied the peaceful and determined face of the young African brother, I was deeply moved, as I was when I later pondered the words of the life commitment. The prayers for the new brother were loving and full of trustful hope. The words of the life vows were simple, but radical. No half-hearted discipleship this. It was a separation from much that the world holds dear but expressed a vision of community which our competitive and fragmented world sometimes holds in contempt. The commitment of a Taizé brother means embracing the cross. But the cross is never lived without the resurrection. They know that, and they are content.

As we drifted away from the short time of prayer, the young brother's commitment will have raised for many there the question of Christian discipleship. Of course this is not surprising. Young people will have on their minds, consciously or otherwise, questions about their future. 'What career should I follow?', 'Will I get married?', 'How can I be sure I'm in love?', 'Where shall I live?', 'What sort of person would I like to be?', 'How can I become more confident in myself?' These questions are all concerned with meaning. Western young people come to Taizé well aware that the cornucopia of life's material riches with which they are blessed, as well as all the opportunities which beckon them, do not automatically promise lives of satisfaction, contentment and fulfilment. There is no guarantee that following one's own personal inclination will lead to a full and rewarding life. There are too many examples of failure around. The pursuit of pleasure and ambition can lead to an empty world where drugs, sex and self-gratification get all mixed up and everything crumbles.

Young people who come from poorer nations may have desires and longings not all that significantly different from their richer friends. Countries emerging from the oppression of Communism or crushed by poverty and war long for freedom and human fulfilment, yet they have found that a culture of drugs and crime is created more easily than a stable economy or a new moral order. Everywhere there is a yearning for 'meaning' but the short cuts to a satisfying life often turn out to be blind alleys.

As I thought about this during my short visit to Taizé the words of Christ in John's gospel riveted my attention: 'I have come that you might have life — and have it in all its abundance.' The abundant life that Christ gives can never be quantified in terms of earthly possessions, or human contentment and happiness, but only in terms of doing his will. And Taizé is a focus for this discovery. In one of the information sheets I was given on arrival I found these words: ' . . . You have come to Taizé to find meaning to your life. One of Christ's secrets is that he loved you first. There lies the meaning of your life: to be loved forever; to be clothed by God's forgiveness and trust. In this way you will be able to take the risk of giving your life.'

We only begin to ask 'What is God's will for me?' when we have come to believe that God is personally interested in us. It's easy to think that we are so insignificant that there is nothing particular in God's relationship with us to be discovered. I've met so many Christians who believe that God has a will for his world, even for his Church, but whose modesty is such that they cannot be convinced that he has a will for them.

Understanding the nature of God's will is far from easy. We cannot see into the mind of God in any case. But the discovery that he loved us first is a personal discovery. Meaning is given to our lives when we realize that God knows and cares for each of us intimately. Jesus said that God's knowledge of us is as close as God's knowledge of the sparrow that perishes or God's numbering of the hairs of our head. Such is God's personal interest, and love for each of us which passes our understanding.

As well as those who need convincing of their significance to God, there are also Christians who seem to comprehend God as their personal possession. Their no doubt innocent assumption is that God is there as a kind of benign 'Jeeves' whose role is to wait on them. I've always been distinctly uncomfortable when I've listened to Christians claiming that they prayed for a parking place on a crowded street and God somehow arranged for one to appear. There was an even more bizarre case I heard about where a couple claimed it was God's will that they were upgraded to business class on an international flight.

What is it, I ask myself, that I object to in these interpretations of God's will? If he is personally interested in us, why shouldn't we expect this kind of divine action?

The reason why I am disturbed by this 'Jeeves' understanding of God is that I believe the will of God has no inherent conflicts within it. If God is 'for us', then he is for all people and for all Christians. As St Paul says, 'God has no favourites'. He doesn't set one up to cast another

117

down. He doesn't give *me* a parking place so that I get to my meeting early but fail to be so courteous to my friend who ends up late. I do believe in the power of prayer but I also believe in the mystery of prayer — and central to mystery is submission to the Father's will in which answered prayer coexists with tragedy and deep darkness. His will for the world is that we live in a unity of love with one another and with him. All that promotes that purpose is in harmony with his will; all that does not, leads away from him.

Austin Farrer once preached a splendid sermon about the will of God, exploring the image of the divine potter moulding us, the clay:

> There is never a moment for the clay when the potter is not doing something with it. God is never standing back and watching us; his fingers are on us all the time . . . If we love his will we take the shape of it. If we are lazy and selfish, his fingers oppose us . . . and crumble us back into obedience. We repent, and without a moment's delay the ever-active fingers are moulding us back into the divine image. (*Said or Sung* [Faith Press, 1960], pp. 80–1)

Those words of Farrer — 'if we love God's will we take the shape of it' — evoked in my mind the prostrate figure of Christ in the garden of Gethsemane. He prayed: 'Not my will but yours be done.' God's will for him took the shape of the cross. But Farrer's rich words also sum up just how Taizé helps people discover God's will for themselves. The journey of discovery is a journey into a discipleship of love. It is God's love which shapes us because his love for us and his will for us cannot be separated. We are invited into a committed relationship of love by him who first loved us. So when we ask 'What is God's will for me?' we should not be searching for some master plan that will provide clear and assured answers for every dilemma we will face. We are instead being called into a committed relationship where our will and God's will become one.

Taizé is itself a 'parable' of commitment. Just as our Lord often spoke in parables, thus answering questions without exhausting their meaning, so Taizé offers stirring examples of people, whose offering of their lives to God can be explored by others. We shall never exhaust the meaning of their offering but we may well be changed and inspired by it.

As Brother Roger and I walked together one evening we explored the meaning of the Community as a 'parable'. 'What is it a parable of?', I asked. 'If a "parable" is meant to draw people closer to the kingdom, in what ways does Taizé do that?'

'There are many different levels to the question' was Brother Roger's response.

'When I was young, I was astonished to see Christians wasting so much energy in justifying their divisions, although they live from a God of love. So in 1940 I understood that it was essential to create a community of men determined to go all the way, through a "yes" for the whole of their life. Living a parable of community meant first of all accomplishing among ourselves on a day-to-day basis the very down-to-earth step of being reconciled every day, in order to be consequent with the Gospel; giving concrete expression in daily life to the vocation to reconciliation, and doing this without delay.' From the beginning, the Community saw itself to be a 'parable' because in this Community genuine reconciliation between Christians and between people of different nationalities and traditions was taking place. 'Above all we wanted to live the spirit of the Gospel: joy, simplicity and mercy.'

And then Brother Roger continued: 'As years went by,

we made an unexpected discovery. Since so many people are far away from the faith at the present time, one of the responsibilities confided to us is to be attentive to so many of the young who are seeking at the sources of faith. When they come to Taizé, they are looking for a meaning to their lives. Some of them begin to ask "What is God's will for my life?" "What is Christ expecting from me?" We are well aware that we communicate the Risen Christ first of all in the times of prayer together. We communicate him also through the sign that our vocation represents by the long fidelities of our existence. Christ calls us to be signs that are quite transparent, quite simple, through our lives. And lo and behold these signs are bearers of Gospel realities through which Christ will leave his imprint on those he entrusts to us. They discover something that is going to resonate within them, not through remaining among us, but in preparing themselves, wherever God leads them, to say a "yes" to his call.'

Our 'yes' to God's call. That simple phrase stayed with me for many hours. Later that evening I asked a young brother what that meant for him. Before joining the Community he had been a medical student. Taizé made such a deep impression on him that he decided to join the Community. Did some people consider that he was running away from life? His answer was swift with a ready smile: 'Of course there must have been some who thought that. They possibly imagined that I tossed away a marvellous and interesting career. But I don't see it that way. Taizé is never an escape from life. All the temptations and demands of life are to be found here. We cannot run away from the cost of living closely together here. The giving up of possessions and the taking upon oneself the commitment to celibacy are not easy. We make the public declarations once in our life but the living out of the promises is a daily event and only sustainable by the grace of God.'

As a parable of community it is natural that Taizé is a place where the nature of a lifelong commitment to God is regularly considered. None of the brothers expects that more than a tiny fraction of the thousands of young people who come will find a vocation to the religious life. Obviously the brothers rejoice when they discover that a young man has been called by God to join the Community. But Taizé does not have a mission for its own growth. Brother Roger is not seeking to establish a world-wide monastic family. In fact he often says that if there are one or two new brothers each year, that is quite enough. Yet Taizé promotes lifelong commitment and consecration to the things of God, and the fact that it is a religious community is vital to an understanding of its impact.

The dozens of brothers robed in white and kneeling in the centre of the Church of Reconciliation are a constant reminder of lifelong commitment. They express through what they are the radical demand of God upon our lives. Young people are drawn by their very wholeheartedness. Nothing is held back in their offering to God, they are a refreshing counter to conventional religion where half-heartedness rather than whole-heartedness seems so prevalent.

I believe the Church as a whole needs its religious orders for that very reason. They remind us of the radical demands of Christian discipleship. They remind us of the priority of prayer. They recall us to a life of simplicity. They witness to the truth that the nuclear family is not the only setting for authentic Christian life. I returned from Taizé more convinced than ever that the Anglican Church needs its religious communities for its life of prayer and mission to grow. I cannot think of a more worthwhile Christian service than to be called to Christ in a religious community.

I recognize, of course, that vocations to the religious life, like vocations to the ordained ministry, are never going to be the normative form of Christian discipleship. Even in the Middle Ages, when the monastic orders were strong, the laity vastly outnumbered the clergy, monks and nuns. So what does Taizé have to say to those whose call will be in the world as teachers, engineers, bank clerks, systems analysts, business women and men, politicians, and university professors? How do we say 'yes' to God's call to serve him in a secular setting?

Even though there are many differences between Taizé and the places where we live and work, the parable of community provides several principles to guide us.

DISCIPLESHIP IS SHAPED BY LOVE

A week at Taizé can be the start of a relationship of love that will last a lifetime. Susan, one of our young English pilgrims, remarked: 'On my first evening here I went to church early to get a good place only to find the church jammed with people who had exactly the same idea. I could not get over the sight of so many young people praying and meditating. As I prayed I found myself caught up in the common prayer and I realized that it was not religion that was the secret of Taizé but love: the love of God and love of people.'

Susan was right. Love is the key to commitment. You don't bind yourself to something you don't love. Love is the foundation of commitment. If we love Christ we will want to follow his will for our lives; we shall desire to use our talents in his service. When the rich young man in the gospels came running to Jesus seeking eternal life, our Lord saw his enormous potential. Mark's gospel states that Jesus 'looking upon him, loved him'. Our Lord then said: 'One thing you lack: go, sell what you have; give to the poor and you will have treasure in heaven; and come follow me.' The challenge was too great. 'He went away sorrowful, for he had great possessions.' His love of his life-style was greater than his love for Christ. His choice took him away from following.

The point of the story is not simply that wealth and riches are wrong. It's that they become idolatrous when they get in the way of Christian discipleship. Wealth may be used by dedicated Christians to the glory of God. But we cannot put our trust in it or think that wealth is a sign of God's blessing. In the Sermon on the Mount Jesus blesses the poor. He offers no comfort for the rich. The rich must throw themselves on his mercy and use their possessions for the good of others as well as for themselves. It is love which transforms what we are and which contains the alchemy which allows our possessions to be aspects of discipleship. As the hymn puts it:

> So, living Lord, prepare us now
> your willing helplessness to share;
> to give ourselves in sacrifice
> to overcome the world's despair;
> in love to give our lives away
> and claim your victory today.
>
> *(Alan Gaunt)*

DISCIPLESHIP IS SAYING 'YES' TO GOD'S CALL
TO FOLLOW HIM

At Taizé everyone is expected to join a group to study the theme of the week. The Community caters for many different possibilities: Bible studies, doctrinal themes, beginners groups, even a silence group which sounded attractive. I sat with the young people and followed through a theme on Christian discipleship. I was struck by how the brother leading the session made the topic so relevant for his audience. The questions he posed were important for them. What is it to follow Christ today? How does the decision to follow him affect our studies, our professional lives, our use of time and our relationships? What are the things that get in the way of being committed to Christ? The pilgrims were encouraged to share their thoughts deeply with one another in these groups.

For John from the north of England a breakthrough came when he realised that it was not the quantity of faith that determined one's journey but the person in whom you were trusting. 'I felt very unworthy about offering my life to God. I knew so little about the Christian faith and at times my doubts are so numerous. But Taizé taught me that my faith was not as important as putting my trust in Christ. With a tiny seed of faith I was able to say "yes" to him and follow him.'

I was able to share John's story with Brother Roger and be remarked that it was typical of the discovery of many young people who come on pilgrimage. 'They arrive with such high expectations even though they may be completely ignorant of our life. They come with ideals and longings that only God can fill. Perhaps they discover from us something to do with "trust" because in a world which constantly lets people down, they arrive at a place which lives on trust — trusting God and trusting one another.' Brother Roger continued: 'It is difficult for people, especially young people, to make a lifelong commitment for Christ. We try to show them that living a life of trusting God means trusting him for this day and then tomorrow. The "yes" forever that we have pronounced in response to his call has to be repeated in our hearts every day and often several times a day. And in the trusting is to be found the grace and strength of God who never lets us down.'

DISCIPLESHIP MEANS IDENTIFYING OUR GIFTS AND OFFERING THEM TO GOD

Taizé is also a place where people discover that they have something to offer God. First, they hit upon the truth that they are not alone in asking fundamental questions about life. They realize at Taizé how universal are these questions of meaning, hope and fulfilment. They are sometimes astonished and encouraged to find that many others too are thinking about the place of God in their lives. This is of particular relevance to young people from the United Kingdom. Somehow young people in England are inhibited from acknowledging that religious questions matter. Taizé gives them an opportunity to see that there is nothing odd in exploring the place God has in your life. It counters the frequent misconception in English views of religion, namely that the Christian faith is a crutch for those without the courage or strength to make their own way in the world.

But there is nothing wimpish about the brothers at Taizé. They are not running away from life's problems. I saw instead a rugged independence of character in many of them. Indeed, the impression given is that being a Christian brings a new maturity because faith has to relate to life. The brothers refuse to entertain the view that a pilgrimage to Taizé is to run away from the world. They resist this by their constant awareness and reference to the problems which confront the human family.

The mixture of backgrounds of people at Taizé is also a parable for some. Sarah, from Liverpool, voiced the opinion of many working-class young people as she remarked: 'People often think that Christianity is for those who come from rich backgrounds and those who talk with a plum in their mouths. But God is for all of us and he takes us as we are and uses us as we are.' For her it was 'listening' to God's voice that drew her to realize that her own sense of inadequacy was getting in the way. She began to understand that she had to allow God to remove the layers of self which stood between him and her real being. She began to feel greatly loved and then felt she could actually start to love herself and to be content with a person with whom God was happy. And from the listening came the longing to be usable. 'I want to serve God somehow', she said determinedly, 'even if it is only washing up I shall do it with all my heart — for him.'

The Community is a model of this, too. The brothers come from all different kinds of backgrounds and nationalities. Not all of them have had the privilege of higher education and not all of them are intellectual high-fliers. That makes no difference. Each brother brings to the Community his own special attributes and experiences and enlarges the whole by his contribution. For Brother Roger living in community is to live by grace: 'All of us are aware that we are the poor of Christ. Yet we also know that God has placed in each human being gifts that are unique. So why do we doubt our gifts so much? And as we compare ourselves with others, why do we wish to have their gifts and to hide away our own? It is as we fully accept our own gifts that we become truly creative.'

But how do we identify our gifts so that we can offer them to God? Perhaps we need to distinguish between developed gifts and latent gifts. Developed gifts are the qualities we now have. Perhaps with the benefit of a good education we are articulate, confident and self-possessed. Our natural bent may be towards science or engineering; or it might be directed towards one of the caring professions. Our gifts sometimes give us clues where we may best serve God. I might want to serve God as an artist. It might be the most compelling thing I can think of. But if I am not blessed with the ability to paint, then it's doubtful if that is God's will for me. If, however, I have discovered in myself a desire to care for those who are sick and it is clear that I have the ability, then that could amount to a call from God to serve him in that way. Whatever we do, we shall want to offer our work to God and seek his blessing. We shall want to be the very best for him and aim for the highest standard we can achieve. We shall not settle for second best. God's call is to do our work joyfully for him, rejoicing in it and aiming to serve him to the best of our ability. Conscientious-ness, honesty, hard graft and a joyful spirit are wonderful qualities to offer him.

Latent gifts are the gifts within us that may become explicit as God uses us in challenging situations. We may dread now doing a certain thing — feeling totally inadequate. But as we grow in commitment to our Lord we may well find that previously undiscovered qualities surface surpris-ingly. 'Grace perfecting human nature' is a well-known experience in the Christian life and one of the many discoveries we make when we submit to God's will and launch on his adventure of discipleship.

But there is always the possibility that young people will feel a call to offer their lives to God in full-time Christian service. It may be to the religious life as exemplified by Taizé. Each community has its own life, rules and approach. Taizé is typical of none of the others. Every young pilgrim who approaches Brother Roger or one of the other brothers is obviously listened to carefully. The brothers are ready to seek with them what God is expecting of them. But the Taizé Community is reluctant to welcome over-eagerly those young people who coming to Taizé believe that at last they have found their vocation. It is a calling which requires considerable prayer, thought and testing. The same applies to other religious communities. It's not a matter of whether someone is 'good enough'. No one is good enough. But you need gifts and abilities, not least perseverance, to live in community. Most of us could not do it, much as we might like to do so. God's will is always related to what we *can* do, not what we cannot. We need, of course, more people to offer themselves for the religious life, but this has to be considered through prayer and by taking time.

Taizé has always inspired some young people to think whether they should be ordained. Again this has to be contemplated with great care. The opportunities of service in the ministry as a deacon or priest are enormous. We need men and women whose lives God has touched with his grace. Taizé is not only a wonderful testing ground of vocation but it is also a splendid model of Christian living. It is sadly true that too many priests have been trained to minister alone. Perhaps the weakness lay in their theological training. Competitive and isolated patterns of ministerial formation can lead to eccentric or isolated ministries. Not so at Taizé. The Community at Taizé is not for individualists but for those who give themselves in love for others.

For Philip, a young priest and friend of mine, Taizé transformed his ministry and reshaped his understanding of community. He is at present chaplain in a public school in the West Country. He wrote these words to me recently:

> Now eight years into country living and of village country life — the question of 'What it means to belong to the church?' is urgent. While the young people are here there is the school community, chapel worship, etc. Yet only a handful of them have a clue about what 'Christian fellowship' means when they go home. Their experience of the 'Church' is the greatest of all challenges — and so often the feedback is negative. This is in great contrast with Taizé. *There* the Church (as Community) is experienced and its universal aspect glimpsed . . .the authenticity of Taizé, the integrity which has always so powerfully struck me, is that never is the reflective style of worship encouraging a kind of Quietism. It is earthed. Half of the brothers *do* live among the poorest of the earth . . . Taizé and its worship taps into the deep longings of the young for peace and justice and trust throughout the earth . . .

DISCIPLESHIP IMPLIES A DAILY FOLLOWING

It is in Luke's gospel that Christ challenges his disciples to follow him and says: 'If anyone would be a disciple of mine, let him deny himself and take up his cross *daily* and follow me' (Luke 9.23). A daily following requires a daily obedience. In one of his letters Brother Roger deals with the hesitations that often arise when people start to think about offering themselves to God. At first they naturally ask: 'How can I possibly keep it up? Can I hold true to promises I make today?' Brother Roger answers these questions in the following way: 'When you begin to understand that this "yes" commits your whole life, you are aware of a great unknown: How can I ever hold true? But no one is built naturally for living the gospel. Faced with Christ's call to give everything, our first response is a prayer: "Give me the gift of giving myself."'

A week spent at Taizé praying, sharing and reflecting on faith is a way of discovering what God desires for our lives. There will be those who will receive a special commission to follow and for them life will never be the same again. But for many of us Taizé will mean a re-commitment of our lives and gifts to his service. For me as Archbishop I confronted yet again the words of the Johannine Christ: 'I have come that you might have life, and have it in all its abundance.' In a busy life, even one concerned for the Church of Jesus Christ, the goal of a full Christian existence may be narrowed by the demands of the institution. Taizé is a wonderful place to get back to basics again. The life of Christ draws us to himself so that we find that in desiring him, we desire his service above all else; a service which is perfect freedom. Whoever we are and whatever our status in the Church or the world, the call to follow must be taken upon oneself daily. Conversion is not simply a 'once-only' event. However dramatic a conversion experience we have had, no Christian can live in the past. There has to be a daily submission and a daily following.

I began this chapter with the image of Taizé as a 'parable of commitment'. On my second day at Taizé Brother Roger invited me to his room. It was large but I was struck by its simplicity — a few icons, a bed in one corner and a table near the window where we had supper, a desk littered with papers, a Bible and a hymn book. That seemed to be all. It was a symbol of a life uncluttered by possessions yet full of the things that really matter. Here was a man full of contentment in Christ which radiates into the Community. He is typical of all the brothers. There are no regrets about leaving everything behind because each brother is convinced that what he has chosen is the very best — Jesus Christ — and he is content. When all the pilgrims leave Taizé what is left behind is a Community witnessing to self-sacrifice offered in love. A parable of the cross and resurrection.

Eight

The journey home

Leaving anywhere where one's experience has been good is always a wrench. Leaving Taizé behind for me and our English pilgrims was sadness indeed. Like Peter on the Mount of Transfiguration many of them wanted to stay 'forever' or, at least, they wanted to retain the experience of Taizé on their return to Britain.

I mention the story of the Transfiguration because at Brother Roger's request I was invited to address the entire Taizé Community on the final Friday of my visit and that became my theme. I drew attention to the wonderful experience that Peter, James and John had when, together with their Lord, they met Moses and Elijah on the Mount. Peter in his usual impulsive way said: 'Lord, it is good to be here. Let me make three booths — one for you, one for Moses and one for Elijah!' He wanted to make the event permanent. This, I suggested, is exactly what we are tempted to do whenever we have great experiences — we want them to last forever. We are keen to frame them or freeze them. We never want to leave them behind. The passage however tells us that the glory burnt so brightly that 'they saw no one but Jesus only'. That, I said, is ever the mission of Taizé. People should not leave the place simply saying: 'What a wonderful place Taizé is!' Rather, the community wants people to meet the living God so that they respond: 'We saw no one but Jesus; we saw our Lord; we caught a fresh glimpse of his love for us.' Like Peter and his fellow disciples, whenever we have such wonderful times we have to leave the mountain top and return to the valley where the Christian faith has to be lived out.

Towards the end of the week I asked several of our young people what Taizé has given them. Here are just some of the responses I recorded at the time.

A young man from the north of England, just about to go up to university, reflected: 'Taizé brought everything together. I had grown up in a lively church and my parents, though not great churchgoers, were very sympathetic. I knew quite a bit about the Christian faith but, I'll have to admit, it was "bits". Taizé made two deep impressions on me. First, I learned something about the breadth of Christianity. I made friends with some Poles of my own age. I was impressed by the naturalness of their walk with God and their love of him. Their devotion shamed my feeble prayer life. I thought to myself one evening as I saw them kneeling for hours in the church: "These people have been through such hardship and have none of the possessions I have — but there is such joy and vitality in their lives and hearts!"

'Second', he continued, 'I really learned to pray at Taizé. Up to that point prayer, for me, was simply a form of words I used whenever I remembered to pray. I used to find it such an effort. When I arrived at Taizé and attended the church for the first time I wondered how I could keep still for so long and when the long silence began I really wondered what there was to think about! Gradually I found myself being still and very comfortable in the presence of God. I did not mind when my thoughts wandered all over the place. I managed to meditate on the short Bible passages. I found the flickering lights around the altar a focus for my prayers and praises. As the week progressed my prayer life deepened so that I wanted to spend longer in prayer.'

For Joanne from the Midlands the pilgrimage was the real start of her Christian life. A girl with sparkling eyes and a ready smile, she had not been a practising Christian for very long. Taizé was a bolt from the blue. She used the expression 'gobsmacked' to describe what Taizé meant to her. 'I started to attend my local church just a few months ago. When I heard about the Archbishop's visit to Taizé a friend said that she would like to go on it. I did not have a clue where Taizé was. When someone said that it was in southern France and it would be very hot and quite cheap I thought it sounded fun! I put my name forward in my church. Then someone said that it was run by a load of monks and it meant attending church every day. I was horrified and wondered what I had let myself in for! But someone said that Taizé was the place where the lovely songs come from. When I heard that I was relieved because I thought that any place which could turn out such great music was bound to be all right — even if it sounded all a little bit religious.'

'So what did you make of the week?' I asked.

Joanne smiled and held up two objects in her hands. One was a large bowl and the other a cassette of Taizé worship. 'I think', she said, 'these two gifts I have just bought from the shop express what I have gained from the community. The bowl will remind me of the fellowship I have enjoyed. I came as an "individual" Christian. I shall return as one who has discovered the Church. The bowl will remind me that I cannot "sup" alone. I need others. Taizé has made me aware of the breadth of the Church and its riches. I met this wonderful Russian priest and his wife — they are so poor but so rich in God. From now on when we say in the Creed "I believe in the holy Catholic Church" I will think of Taizé and the Roman Catholics, the Orthodox, the Lutherans, the Calvinists and the Anglicans I met there.'

Then taking a deep breath she handed me the cassette of Taizé worship. 'I love music', she said. 'When I first started going to our village church I could not but help notice the music of Taizé when sung by the choir. It was meditative, reflective and haunting. I've never been able to understand Latin but singing a few Latin words, or other languages I did not know, did not get in the way of worshipping God. If anything it helped to sing in a strange language to God who is beyond words in any case. I was "gobsmacked" by the worship at Taizé. The rich sound of several thousand people singing; the deep silence in prayer. And, you know', she interrupted herself, 'the way Taizé makes you think about the church by going beyond the Church!'

I asked her to explain herself. 'I mean that Taizé is clearly "churchy" but it takes us beyond usual definitions of what a church means to ordinary people.' Joanne went on to say that before coming to Taizé, she thought of a church as a place with pews, with solemn services and a choir singing traditional music. She continued: 'I must admit I thought of church buildings as cold and dull places — full of history and pointing back into a past that we shall never know fully about. But Taizé is nothing like that. You sit on the floor, you can relax. Taizé invites you to be yourself. There is no formal liturgy, as such. It is very simple and plain — and yet, rich, exciting in its "ordinariness" and plain in its variety and difference. It is all so difficult to put into words.'

But what about archbishops and other clergy who come with young people on pilgrimage? While, of course, Taizé has a special ministry to young people it is not only for them. It would be wrong to consider Taizé 'a place for young people only'. Many older people have been helped and challenged through the spirituality of this place. The brothers are not all young — several of them are Brother Roger's age and a number in middle age. Age is no barrier at Taizé. Those of us wanting to know more about God and eager to deepen our Christian experience will find Taizé a place of deep challenge and inner renewal. For myself, leading a large world-wide communion with many opportunities but also many problems to resolve, Taizé brought its own challenges and its own distinctive contribution to bear. I found my daily conversations with the various brothers inspiring and challenging. We were in many respects kindred spirits. We shared the same longing to see the Church of Jesus Christ blazing with new life. We shared the same theological vision that prayer and spirituality are basic to evangelism and Christian formation. We desired in different ways to see the reconciliation of all Christians. I saw in Brother Roger, and indeed in all the brothers, the working out of the radical claims of Jesus Christ. They challenged me, without realizing it, to examine my prayer life, to cast out the busy and fretful spirit, to spend more time listening and less time asking, to spend more time adoring and thanking and less time worrying, to spend more time trusting and daring and less time wondering and questioning. They helped me to look afresh at my priorities and to wonder at the daily providence of God who always nourishes and provides. Taizé was an oasis in which my wife and I were able to relax physically and mentally and to have a rare opportunity to reflect on the many challenges which confront me as Archbishop. Perhaps most delightful was the fact that I had no special role as leader; I was there *with* young people to share in a common pilgrimage.

But Taizé also presents the Church, as well as the individual, with a challenge which must be confronted. It is the challenge for all communions which bear the name of Christ to be *truly* communities rooted in Christ.

In one form Taizé refreshingly 'subverts' the formal church by confronting us with our true identity. We know when we get there that the real heart of 'church' is found in simplicity, adoration, prayer and worship. We find ourselves with other Christians of different traditions and the practice of worshipping with them makes it impossible for us to deny their authenticity as Christians. We are faced with the implications of a common baptism and the sadness that we cannot as yet meet around a common table in Holy Communion. Taizé therefore makes us stare at our divisions and the things which force us apart. This, of course, is both its objective and its task. The Community is a community of reconciliation: its role is to lead others to Christ and therefore to one another. As Jürgen Moltmann, the Lutheran theologian, puts it splendidly: 'The nearer we come to Christ, the nearer we come together.' This too is Taizé's vocation, for it is a Christ-centred community whose centripetal force helps to make us one. For so many young Christians ecumenism, has been shaped by Taizé and deepened by the encounter with other Christians of differing traditions. This meeting in worship, prayer, Bible study, discussion groups and through eating and being together, enables Taizé to share its ecumenical vision with fresh generations of young people, thus gradually, gently and perceptibly changing the way we see one another.

The real face of the Church is also found as worship is encountered in simple beauty. The word 'simplicity' has run through this book. People return from Taizé saying: 'It is so simple and basic!' So it is — and therein lies its strength. By being simple Taizé becomes accessible to so many: we all feel we can belong there. But it is simple in another sense: the heart of Christianity is found there. It challenges our patterns of worship and says: 'Yes, formal worship and indeed grand worship is all very well — indeed, we do not criticize it — but sit, kneel, stand and do not feel that anyone is asking you to conform. And when you pray, you are not compelled to share in interminable liturgies or make great statements of faith. Simply come as you are with an open and empty heart — and our Lord can fill it.'

But this is not usually what institutional Christianity says to people these days. The complexity and formality of worship can put people off the Church and alienate them from the heart of the faith. The word that young people often use of church worship is 'boring'. No one can say that of Taizé but neither can they say it is a circus or that it is there simply to pander to the emotions. Worship that demands silence, meditation, thought and waiting upon God is not the religion of ecstatic revivalism. Because the form is straightforward, the music gloriously beautiful as well as lucid, the manner of worship unencumbered by complicated ceremonial, people of all ages do feel that it speaks to them. I cannot underline sufficiently the challenge that Taizé presents to us today. We simply dare not fail our generation by presenting worship in such a way that whole generations are alienated from the life of the Church because of the coldness and aridity of traditional or even modern forms.

What is the answer? It is curious that often we believe the answer to lie simply in 'bringing Christianity up to date'. We strip away traditional models, cast away the ecclesiastical garb and replace it with a bareness and straightforwardness that we feel modern people require and desire.

Taizé encourages us to think again. Young people are not crying out for the removal of movement, beauty, mystery, colour and light. Taizé, indeed, revels in such elements. There is the dignity of movement as the white-robed brothers enter. There is the tradition of kneeling, bowing and the use of the sign of the cross. There are formal prayers and above all the repetitive and evocative singing of psalms and songs. Atmosphere is very important at Taizé but it is not the engineered and deliberately orchestrated atmosphere reminiscent of the theatre. Instead, the ambience is of a devotion centred on God, sensitive to the needs of all worshippers.

A few months after returning from the pilgrimage I received this letter from a young man, Joe, who had been on the Taizé trip.

Dear Archbishop . . . you will remember that we had a talk about our youth club and the difficulties of getting them along to the Sunday evening service. They all complained that it wasn't for them; that the grown-ups did not talk to them, that the worship was foreign to their experience and that it did not speak to them. Well, when I returned I thought that Jane and I should share our experience with them, as you suggested. So this is what we did. We decided to share an act of Taizé worship with our group of twelve young people. We bundled into a small room at the back of the church hall. We sat on cushions or on the floor. I started

by teaching them a few Taizé chants and once we had gone
over them a few times the simple service began. On a table
we placed some candles and in darkness we prayed in
silence, someone read a short passage of Scripture, we
meditated upon it, we sang some more Taizé songs and had
some guided meditation. Everyone agreed that it was
brilliant . . .

What that young man was expressing was the importance
of young people having some moments when the Christian
faith is stated in cultural forms appropriate to their life. We
older Christians often forget that when people come to
church the unspoken cultural message we convey is
'conform to us'. We, the dominant group, assume that
young people are comfortable with the dress, expectations,
language and expressions of the receiving fellowship.
However young people have their own culture with its own
values, expressions and language. Joe may not have realized
it but what he was doing was introducing his friends to the
Christian tradition by using its essential tools — prayer,
silence, Bible reading and song — without the 'clutter' of
the dominant culture getting in the way. Later perhaps
they will be able also to take something from that dominant
culture but only when they are ready for it. In the
meantime Joe and his friends are discovering renewal in
worship for themselves. That is a significant contribution
which Taizé is offering to contemporary Christianity.

The day before we all left to return home I met up with
all the diocesan co-ordinators to discuss what we had gained
together and to reflect upon the experience of the pilgrimage.
They shared their experiences and the many discussions
they had had with their young adults. We agreed that it had
been a marvellous and uplifting time for us all. We older

Christians had gained so much from what we had learned
from Taizé and our young people.

'But what of the future?' I asked. 'How can we build
upon this rich event? What lessons does it hold for our
Church?'

We shared our concerns about the lamentable failure of
so many churches which have no youth policy and, indeed,
no young people. Only one in five churches have any form
of youth activity. In many cases no Sunday schools exist. A
shameful story in a church which pioneered the Sunday
school movement. We had heard young people say, time
and again, that they felt so alone in churches where others
were over the age of forty. From such worries as this,
expressed with such feeling by young Christians who ached
to belong, the alarming problem facing the Church became
transparent. What chance was there of holding such loyal
young Christians, we wondered, if young people felt so
marginalized?

It was also recognized that the challenge facing the
Church was to put young people far higher up its agenda.
Are we putting our best lay people into supporting young
people's work and encouraging them? Are we giving them
space to feel valuable in our worship? Are they on our
Parochial Church Councils, do we ask them to take part in
reading lessons, saying prayers and taking other responsibilities? Are we willing to let them, on occasions, lead a
youth service in church and be there to encourage them?
How much money is devoted to Sunday school and youth
events, we wondered? The priorities of a church are often
gleaned from the church's accounts at the end of the
financial year. What we spend our money on is usually a
good guide to what we value most.

Young people can of course be very demanding and often

fickle. They can be noisy, demonstrative and critical. They sense when they are despised, unwelcome and unwanted. A number of young adults said that they believed their clergy feared them. 'He is scared of me', one young man said, 'I think he is afraid of young people and the challenge we represent.' What a pity if clergy feel like this. If only they could see that young people are an untapped source of energy, vitality and creativity which could add greatly to the life of the Church. Young people are not to be feared but loved. They are people made in the likeness of God who have to be tenderly won for our Lord.

The secret which Taizé teaches us is fourfold. First, *young people respond to warmth and affection.* Hypocrisy they will see miles away and despise, but genuine devotion will always provoke a positive reaction. It doesn't matter if the adult who gives it is far older, reflecting the traditions of a past generation. Love is the key quality which will encourage young people to trust and value any person who works alongside them. Seeing Brother Roger, or other brothers, with young people at Taizé demonstrates this. The ease with which they are accepted by young adults illustrates the point that above all else the brothers want the young to share the love of God which they already share. Young adults will be contemptuous of all insincere efforts to copy their speech and dress, as if that is the way to get on their wavelength.

A second element is to *value the qualities and insights which young adults bring to church life.* There is a refreshing honesty and sharpness which they will always contribute. Social etiquette may well disguise the true feelings of older people — not so young people. There is a directness and trans-parency about them which is often disconcerting but always very revealing. They are not looking to overturn every tradition the Church has but they will want to know: 'What does it mean? What does it signify? Why are you doing it that way?' They will question empty radicalism; signs and symbols with meaning they are prepared to accept.

This indeed is a door through which we may enter to share the riches of Christianity with young people. When young people start to experiment with worship they will need to use symbols. Some they will bring from their own culture. But on hand is the language of symbols, sacraments and signs which the Christian faith supplies in abundance and which can be adapted to their culture. It is this dimension which Taizé has explored with success over the years: evocative language, the use of light, song and sound. Much more could be done by older Christians in exploring the imagery which young people employ to make sense of the world around them. We sometimes fail young people by our lack of imagination.

A third element is that of *participation*. Young adults hate being spectators. They like to get involved in things. Taizé uses young people — whether it be peeling potatoes for 3,000 people, tidying up the dormitories, caring for others, taking part in a discussion group or, for that matter, being entrusted with responsibility for a delicate mission somewhere in Eastern Europe or elsewhere. Young people who come to Taizé know from the way things are run that the place does not cosset them by supplying their every want; it is a place in which they genuinely participate. Because they feel involved they feel valued and important. Taizé is an example too that young adults are not bored by reflective styles of worship or put off by silence or contemplation. The reverse is the case. When they are held by worship their powers of concentration and their desire to meet with the living God are not inferior to those of older Christians.

At another level Taizé identifies with many of the concerns that bother young adults these days. It is interesting how often environmental matters and questions of justice and peace surface at Taizé. While it is true that young people will bring many of these important issues with them, they find at Taizé that the questions are not extraneous to the community but essential to its commitment to the world. This of course is not surprising to those who know the history of Taizé because the original vision Brother Roger had arose from his concern for reconciliation and his compassion for the poor and needy, the helpless and hopeless. Young people will always respond when other Christians share their concerns and especially when the evidence is that direct involvement in political and social action from a Christian perspective is encouraged.

The fourth element is that young people do *respond to genuine spirituality*. Older people are often put off by what they consider to be young people's obsession with relevance. That may well be the superficial face of young adults today. Often this disguises many deeper concerns. Many of them are asking questions about the meaning and purpose of life. They are searching for fulfilment and the question of God is never far away from their thoughts. Too often, sadly, they retreat from the really important questions, put off by institutional Christianity or by school religion or by the behaviour of those who represent the Christian faith. In my many years of working with young people, not only in universities but also from working-class estates, I have become convinced of their profound quest for a vital spirituality. They react positively to adults who treat them as intelligent and developing people. Taizé's experience of working with young adults confirms this. Their devotion in prayer, their questions and their attitude to life, affirm the depths of spirituality which they have and of which they are capable. We fail them only when we question their spiritual breadth and judge them by our standards.

The week-long pilgrimage over, the pilgrims left the quiet hillsides of southern Burgundy to return to the normality of daily life in England. They returned to homes where in the majority of cases their Christian experience is not shared. They returned to churches where in so many cases young people are 'put up with' rather than prized, valued and loved. As they left I thought of the enthusiasm and ability which they represented and the latent possibilities that God could see in each one of them. Without doubt the majority of them had been profoundly moved and influenced by the pilgrimage to Taizé. But what fruit would it produce, I wondered, in the days ahead?

Reflecting on this I asked for this letter to be read to all the young people on the coaches on the long return journey home:

Dear Fellow Pilgrim

As you return home I want to express my thanks to you all for coming with me to Taizé. It has been a very special week in my life — and I hope for you too. As we return home, what are the specific challenges that face us?

First, let me remind you that your Pilgrimage has not stopped. The Christian life is a pilgrimage — a journey with God through all the hazards and difficulties of life. Let us all be committed to our God and his Church. Take home with you the story of what Taizé has given you — but don't live in the past and rely on past experiences. Live out your faith in the world. Second, I have listened to some of you telling me how lonely you feel in your churches. This makes me more determined than ever to support work among young people and to show that the Christian faith is still relevant to young and old alike. Will you join me in that commitment? The best witnesses to Christian faith amongst young people are young people themselves. I hope that Taizé will have given you confidence to overcome shyness about your faith. Be an enthusiast for Christ! Our joint enthusiasm could make all the difference. Don't forget to ask for an opportunity to report on the Pilgrimage and to tell your congregation what a challenge the whole experience has been . . . So back to the ordinariness of our lives — but now transfigured through Christ who goes down the mount with us to serve others. Enjoy your Christianity and share it with others.

So now more than a year after the memorable visit to Taizé the experience continues with all of us who went. I still receive letters that encourage me, like, for example, that from the young man who at Taizé felt that God was calling him to the ordained ministry and who is now about to test his vocation. Then there was the mother who wrote to say that her son went on the pilgrimage very reluctantly, as he was at the time going through a violent anti-church phase. She wrote to say that he had returned transformed and that his Christian commitment was 'heart-deep'. Then there is the letter from the clergyman who said that his youth club had grown three times through the zeal of six members of his church who came on the pilgrimage. Such stories could be multiplied; all witness to the remarkable ministry of the brothers.

It is only right, then, that Brother Roger should have the last word. To him and his Community belong the vision which helped to found this important and inspiring work.

Their devotion, spirituality and infectious faith continue to influence and transform the life of institutional Christianity. Long may it do so.

Brother Roger writes these challenging words in *His Love Is a Fire:* 'That communion which is the Church interests us, not for itself, but certainly when it stimulates us to search for God at the wellsprings of adoration, when it prompts us to live Christ for others, and when it becomes a place of communion for the whole of humanity.'